Rusty Anchors

Nancy Foltz Beck

NANCY FOLTZ BECK

BALBOA.PRESS
A DIVISION OF HAY HOUSE

Copyright © 2021 Nancy Foltz Beck.

All rights reserved. No part of this book may be used or reproduced by any means, graphic, electronic, or mechanical, including photocopying, recording, taping or by any information storage retrieval system without the written permission of the author except in the case of brief quotations embodied in critical articles and reviews.

Balboa Press books may be ordered through booksellers or by contacting:

Balboa Press
A Division of Hay House
1663 Liberty Drive
Bloomington, IN 47403
www.balboapress.com
844-682-1282

Because of the dynamic nature of the Internet, any web addresses or links contained in this book may have changed since publication and may no longer be valid. The views expressed in this work are solely those of the author and do not necessarily reflect the views of the publisher, and the publisher hereby disclaims any responsibility for them.

The author of this book does not dispense medical advice or prescribe the use of any technique as a form of treatment for physical, emotional, or medical problems without the advice of a physician, either directly or indirectly. The intent of the author is only to offer information of a general nature to help you in your quest for emotional and spiritual well-being. In the event you use any of the information in this book for yourself, which is your constitutional right, the author and the publisher assume no responsibility for your actions.

Any people depicted in stock imagery provided by Getty Images are models, and such images are being used for illustrative purposes only. Certain stock imagery © Getty Images.

Print information available on the last page.

ISBN: 978-1-9822-6523-6 (sc)
ISBN: 978-1-9822-6522-9 (hc)
ISBN: 978-1-9822-6534-2 (e)

Library of Congress Control Number: 2021904625

Balboa Press rev. date: 03/16/2021

CONTENTS

Preface vii
Acknowledgments ix

Chapter 1   Harold W. Foltz, S1, USN 1
Chapter 2   Home Is Where the Anchor Drops 9
Chapter 3   Yong Man—Big Suplize 13
Chapter 4   Settlin' on the Liu 17
Chapter 5   Garden of Delights 23
Chapter 6   Lovin' Lui 27
Chapter 7   Chi-Foo-Sung 31
Chapter 8   Made in China 37
Chapter 9   Only Time Will Tell 41
Chapter 10 Nightmares and Prayers 47
Chapter 11 Clarity at Sea 55
Chapter 12 One Dock at a Time 61
Chapter 13 Shabby Chic 65
Chapter 14 Cookin' at Sea 69
Chapter 15 No Crib for a Bed 75
Chapter 16 Impromptu Catastrophes 83
Chapter 17 The Easy Way Out 93
Chapter 18 Pals Forever 99
Chapter 19 Uncle Sam's Son 107
Chapter 20 One Enchanted Evening 111
Chapter 21 House of Madelaine 117
Chapter 22 The Buddy They Loved 129

Chapter 23	Voices in the Fog	131
Chapter 24	Agnes of Oakland	135
Chapter 25	Need a Lift?	141
Chapter 26	Paddlin' Madelaine	149
Chapter 27	"That's My Daddy!"	155
Chapter 28	The Bouncing Baby Bottle	161
Chapter 29	Pride and Promises	167
Chapter 30	Larry the Leaper	171
Chapter 31	Private Party	179
Chapter 32	Mamma and the Met	189
Chapter 33	The Hill to Hell	193
Chapter 34	Sally Sue Snoots	199
Chapter 35	Popcorn and Petting	207
Chapter 36	Bodacious Nanna	211
Chapter 37	Wooden Marshmallows	221
Chapter 38	Simply Family	229
Chapter 39	Open for Business	233
Chapter 40	Cricket Was in Love	237
Chapter 41	Rusty Anchors	241

Chaplin's Letter, Florida, 2000 247

PREFACE

I affirm life is a series of memories, mementos, and reminiscences strung together as the seasons of our lives. In theory, the passing of time supplies additional lights and ornaments until the creation is complete in some elusive era. My experiences with Mamma and the chief exemplified that belief. Baby David and I were born in the war years and lived a somewhat nomadic life typical of dependents of active-duty military personnel.

Frequent relocations required shifts in attitudes, methodologies, responsibilities, and friendships—as well as men and women of extraordinary courage and perseverance. Military wives have always provided comfort while rocking the cradles of normalcy in his absence. They are courageous, loving companions and mothers, skilled as an admiral, knowing and fulfilling equal but different responsibilities within the home. She more firmly grasps the scepter of responsibility during times of deployment.

To every military wife, mother, and family, I express admiration and understanding. To my children, grandchildren, and future posterity, I affirm that life's uncertainties and possibilities are an essential part of growth. It is hoped that reading these stories of yesterday's experiences will empower one to connect and recouple with exceptional ancestors who made our lives and freedoms a reality.

To my husband, Lt JG Stanley P. Beck (Ret), and my dear brother Petty Officer David H. Foltz, I express gratitude for bravery and dedication during distraught times. I desire to share personal experiences of yesterday, of family life, lived—and missed. These stories and musings shaped our lives and influenced who we became, the parents and grandparents we are. As former dependents, now in our senior years, we realize we weren't alone. Other military families had unique and similar experiences. Our posterities will never know our family stories, our histories, unless we write them—how, during the war years, we were affected by infrequent communications through radio, newsreels, personal letters, and newspaper accounts unless we record them. Lest we forget, we were never alone. We are proud of being military families of a bygone era.

ACKNOWLEDGMENTS

Through the years of compiling this work, many individuals provided invaluable assistance, information, and encouragement. The author sought direction for assembling information meant to enlighten and encourage family members and other readers to appreciate the past sacrifices more fully.

Special thanks extend to friends and family who have given invaluable assistance in the compilation of *Rusty Anchors* and have generously shared their knowledge of military history, editing, computer assistance, and all other aspects required to create this book. The author extends a special debt of gratitude to the following:

David H. Foltz, USN
Janel Reyneke, EdD, first editor
Stanley P. Beck, Lt. USNR, consultant
Larry Wintersteen, BA, MA, CMT, author
Rupert Reyneke, research and design, cover
Yvonne M. Pasquali, software developer and author
Pete Pasquali IV, computer tech and author

Harold at eighteen (1934)

CHAPTER 1
Harold W. Foltz, S1, USN

I've seen it with my own eyes!

*Huangpu (Wang-Pu) The Mother River
Shanghai, China, 1938*

Seaman First Class Harold W. Foltz wiped the sweat from his brow and meticulously followed orders, shoveling dirty black coal into the boilers, doing his best to conform to life in a foreign land. He never dreamed he'd be so far from home and couldn't recall the recruiter saying, "Join the navy, collect two hundred dollars, and go directly to China!" But the twenty-three-year-old was doing his best to adjust. He was a stickler for discipline and proud to be part of a tight-knit crew of sailors.

In the off-hours, Hal often stood at the rail of the ship and watched with rapt attention as Oriental life bustled on Shanghai's principal waterway—deep and wide, the Huangpu River teemed with activity. He was even becoming adept in the use of chopsticks and exploring the city's unfamiliar sites.

It was late afternoon aboard the large, gray ship, and Hal's psyche was humming in neutral. Engaged in his labors, he recalled images of young boys chasing fireflies on warm, muggy Ohio evenings, the smell of rich, fertile farm fields, grassy green knolls, and the unmistakable fragrance of his mother's roses. He thought of Jonny, his only sibling. Neither of the boys was so young these days.

Hal's little brother was a bright, sensitive young man. In the absence of their parents, Hal assumed responsibilities for himself and Jon. Hal was more than just a big brother. He was Jonny's self-appointed guardian, trusted friend, and confident. He made sure Jon finished high school before joining up and sometimes wished he'd done the same for himself. At eighteen, the proud young teenager followed Hal's example of patriotism and enlisted in the military—the US Merchant Marines. Now, there they were—floating on different oceans, worlds apart.

Hal wondered if somewhere out there, Jon might be thinking of him, of glowing insects—and yesterday's brother-chatter.

"Hal, Hal! On the double, hit the deck!" bellowed an agitated sailor. "You gotta see this! You won't believe your eyes!"

Nobody referred to Harold as Hal except the crew. He supposed he was getting used to it, but the sudden, startling sounds jarred him to reality. Shipmates were suddenly scrambling up metal ladders hand over hand, asking questions, surmising answers, and becoming more animated with each step.

"What's goin' on up there?" yelled a busy chief from below deck. Nobody had immediate answers for him. Topside, agitated sailors were ready for a fight. The fervor was infectious and growing. Handrails were packed with white-capped sailors in denim blues, waving their fists in the air and yelling. All military eyes were fixed on a long wooden dock as the sailors tumbled over one another, trying to get a better view.

"Hal, did you bring your binoculars?" asked a shipmate.

"Yeah, Pasquali," came the reply. "These days, I keep 'em real handy." Hal hefted them to his eyes and stood breathless, his mouth agape, clearly transfixed by the commotion in the water below. Unbelievable!

"That chow in my gut ain't doin' me no favors," he muttered grimly, "and it's makin' me woozy. I gotta keep it down, but it's ricey-dicey if I can …"

"Chum over the rail, pal, but don't puke on my deck," growled a nearby sailor. "I got the duty, and I just finished swabbing it. In this heat, I ain't in no mood for doin' it again."

Hal swallowed hard, his eyes still glued to the river below. "Just keep your mouth shut," he told himself.

"Gimme them binoculars," said Hal's shipmate. "I hope what I'm seein' ain't really what I'm seein'. Lemme get a good look." Hal shared his glasses momentarily, then retrieved them for his use. The men were hoping for a case of mistaken reality, but the dreadful truth was staring them in the face. Trouble was brewing with a higher intensity as more and more sampans tied up in the busy waterway. The sailors were clearly livid!

"Too bad this ain't no turkey shoot," bellowed an irate seaman. Shaking his fists at the Chinamen below, the sailor roared, "Getaway, you dirty scum. Leave 'em alone! Get away from those kids!"

A ruckus of any kind always brought the brass topside. Not surprisingly, it seemed every new day's troubles were worse than the day before.

"Make room for me, sailor," ordered the chief. "The cap'n wants to know what's causing the hubbub." The chief glanced over his shoulder as a tall, balding officer stood behind him. The man asked, "What's goin' on down there, bos'n?"

With the crew making so much noise, the chief struggled to give a cohesive reply. It was impossible to make sense of the high-pitched words and incomplete sentences stumbling from the mouths of the enraged sailors.

"I said, what's goin' on, chief?"

"Well, I—I'm not sure yet, Cap'n. There's another commotion dockside. This time it appears to be involving kids in some kind of bamboo cages! I just climbed topside myself, and I can't seem to get a straight answer outta nobody."

The irritated chief grumbled, "Don't you men have anything better to do than stare at a bunch of coolies bringin' a slew a fish or produce ashore? Never seen a sampan before?"

Every day, the brass did their best to ignore dealings on the mainland. They knew if it wasn't US Navy–related, it was none of their business. They reckoned everything out of the navy's jurisdiction was someone else's headache—and they eagerly yielded. But this afternoon, all eyes darted between the officers, crew, the pier, and the heavily loaded sampans bobbing in the water.

Pointing to the long, narrow dock, the animated men, all yelling over one another, turned to the senior officers. One exclaimed, "Sirs, sirs, look at them cages! That ain't no produce they're movin'. Look! Look how heavy they are! Takes a couple of coolies to heft some of 'em. Hear that cryin'? There's kids in them traps—real live children! And the coolies are stackin' 'em on top a one another like they was grocery boxes! They got them kids trapped and scared to death. Nothin' good's goin' on down there."

"Bos'n, pass me the binoculars. I'd like to get a better view for myself," commanded the captain. He knew the massively enraged sailors were more than just Uncle Sam's nephews. Many were young fathers used to American civilities and customs. Anything to do with cruelty to kids—any kids—touched raw nerves. Dressed in a sweaty shirt, a burly, fist-shaking fireman from the boiler room snarled through his teeth. He made vulgar gestures at the coolies on the dock with life-threatening rage, and the "salute" was quickly returned.

"Them fish heads are up to no good. I know it in my bones," Hal said grimly.

"Over there, Hal! Look at 'em people hurrying to the dock!"

A sudden bevy of Chinamen, some in long black robes, feverishly shuffled to the site. Perhaps they were merchants, fishermen, or middlemen brokering on the black market. It was apparent every man was eager to be first, ahead of the crowd. Undaunted by the commotion, indifferent sampan workers continued off-loading another dozen or so bamboo cages. The apparent boss men released the latches, and, one by one, shivering youths crawled or were dragged from the cramped containers. Traumatized, scantily clad, and malnourished, the brood cringed, huddled together, and shook in fear.

Hal stood in shock with his binoculars glued to his eyes. "That one—I think it's a boy—clingin' to that little kid next to him, screamin', panicked, tryin' to hide behind the tall, thin youth in rags. Maybe they're brothers, friends, or total strangers. It really doesn't matter. It's plain; they're scared out of their wits," he murmured.

Wearing ragtag odds and ends, the kids were old before their time. Hal stared in grim consternation as the children attempted to huddle together. Was there no hope for even a grain of decency, protection, or comfort? In fierce anger, the taskmasters shouted and dragged the youths apart. The demands and hand signals indicated the kids were to line up in some sort of order. Tearfully, the anxious children exchanged gazes between the noisy, angry sailors and the brutal coolies demanding instant, blind obedience.

Harold muttered, "I'd like to jump ship and beat their heads in. I'd tear their stinkin' carcass apart. I—I want some kind of justice for them little kids!"

The line was almost straight as the boss men drove the chattel onto the street for public display. Members of the babbling crowds pried open small mouths and examined deciduous teeth or the lack thereof. The absence of decay was a bargaining chip. Unfeeling but curious buyers evaluated the emaciated lot. With calculative acumen, they may as well have been inspecting cattle or sheep for sale in an open market.

The sight was shockingly incredible—trafficking in human flesh. At the auction, sellers displayed their wares in public, gripping them by the hair or skinny little arms, oblivious to their frightened cries. Though the children's terror was palpable, it didn't seem to matter to the eager crowd. When bidding commenced, raucous transactions were quick and heated. Back-and-forth quibbling—and, just like that, it was over. Smiling vendors released their cargo with obvious monetary pleasure and inspected the dirty, tainted yuan in their hands.

These were serious profiteers. Unbelievably, only the money seemed to matter as it passed back and forth among buyers and sellers. As luck would have it, the day had been lucrative. It was gut-wrenching to watch the unappreciated cargo carted away like a pack of scrawny stray dogs. With equal pageantry, buyers gloated over bargained-for merchandise. Shading their squinty eyes from the fading sun, brokers on the dock chattered Oriental jibber-jabber, and smirking vendors chuckled as they restacked the silent, empty crates. They'd be back. Most regrettably, there would be others.

Hal dropped the binoculars to his chest and let them hang from his neck as he stared into space. Brooding, he wiped more sweat with the back of his shaking hand. He knew. They all knew. Slaves, that's what those kids were—helpless little nobodies. No one even tried to save the vulnerable victims.

Hal blended into the muttering pack of shuffling, guilt-ridden sailors and wandered below deck, still pondering the sight.

Nobody wanted them—no mothers, no fathers, nobody. What kind of people half starve their own kind and then sell them for money? Why, water buffalo got the better treatment! An embittered voice in Hal's head screamed, *Shut up, Foltz! Shut up and mind your own business. You can't do nothin'—nothin' for them kids ... nothin'!*

In shock, he felt powerless and angry. Sickened, Hal raced to the cool steelhead just in time to spill what was left of his chow.

Gratingly, he admitted to himself, "I don't even wanna guess what's gonna happen to 'em." His head was pounding, and he felt disoriented as ghosts of the past covered him with a cloak of sorrow, rage, and rejection. He tried to harden himself against the memories. Who cared? They were just little nobodies—nonentities too good for this world. It seemed they were climbing to heaven through the bamboo gates of hell. The everyday spectacles and continual acts of brutalism were bitter. Unfortunately, scuttlebutt said it wasn't going to be over anytime soon.

The chaplain's soft, familiar voice should have calmed Hal's soul, but it did not. "God rest them," the chaplain whispered grimly. "You doing OK, son?"

Hal wiped the vomit from his mouth with the back of his hand, but the smell of it made him sick all over again. He turned to see a man standing behind him, leaning against the wall with his arms folded. The chaplain pulled out a handkerchief, blew his nose—then leaned against the wall again, crossing his legs at the ankles.

"These are hard times, difficult circumstances. I believe we're witnessing history in the making," the chaplain prophetically said. "We've just gotta man up and accept what we can't change. My faith tells me God sees everything."

Harold hoped God was close enough to hear and see the injustices the rest of the crew witnessed.

"Sir, this thing's over my head," Hal replied with as much respect as he could muster. "I ain't into this kidnapping/slave business. Those innocent kids—they ain't done nothin' to deserve this, and here we are, the finest navy in the world, a crew of first-rate flag wavers just lettin' it happen 'n' watchin' it firsthand—doin' nothin' ... nothin' but watchin' them Japs tearin' this country apart."

"This is a land of chaos," replied the nodding chaplain. "We're not here to interfere. We just can't. God sees these atrocities, and because of rape and other barbarous acts, mixed-race kids pay the ultimate price. They're killed or forced out of isolated villages because neither race will accept them. It would seem the attacking entrepreneurs sense the smell of easy money. Labeled problem kids, the children were abandoned, die, or hauled off and sold to get rid of 'em. It's hard to know if those slave kids are the lucky ones or not. Those despicable traffickers are savage devils! I'm sure heaven weeps for the innocent children."

Harold was cleaning himself up—slapping cold water on his flushed face, trying to put his psyche together—when a loudspeaker overhead made a cracking sound:

"Attention, all hands. This is the captain speaking. I, uhm, have every confidence in our abilities to handle the—uhm—strange customs, uhm—unusual circumstances, and events witnessed in this foreign port today. As you know, gentlemen, we represent the finest, free-est nation in the world, here by official invitation of the Chinese government. I'm—uhm—I'm reminding you again, gentlemen, we have absolutely no right to interfere in the internal affairs of this or any other sovereign nation and—or the—maltreatment of citizens of any age. None whatsoever. Let me reiterate, gentlemen, we *will* respect our host countrymen regardless of our personal feelings! Now—uhm—what we witnessed this afternoon was—uhm—unfortunate and part of an ongoing conflict between two nations. And—uhm—the unfortunate children of mixed blood are—uhm—not recognized or accepted by either country. Many are orphans." There was a long pause. "Gentlemen, you will remember we are guests—*guests*—and at all costs and in every circumstance, we will maintain professionalism and neutrality. That will be all, gentlemen. You may resume your duties."

Click.

CHAPTER 2

Home Is Where the Anchor Drops

Shanghai, 1939

In Hal's mind, the horrors of enslaving unwanted, defenseless children harmonized with the rest of the atrocities occurring across the vast, confusing Orient. He noted how routinely it had become to observe lifeless bodies in the river, bobbing seaward like unwanted driftwood. Pathetically, not even the ancient Huangpu tried to hide its shame. Why, just that very morning, another flotilla rode the currents past the ship into oblivion. Once it reached the open sea, God only knew what became of them. It was more than disconcerting to casually observe the freakish lack of civilities or marginalization of human life. Yet, every day, travelers hardly noticed—no use asking questions. Nobody had cogent answers for grisly queries, just shallow justifications—chitchat for excuses.

Hal had been in China long enough for his gut to burn hotter than the coal he shoveled. He hoped it was only the spicy foods, but it seemed to be getting worse. Agonizing over unalterable matters of life and death fanned the flames. Regardless, Hal vowed never to forget the echoes and violence that typified the dreadful underbelly of China. He thought of the auction, the children. How could they be the lucky ones? He guessed it was because they were alive—if one stretched the truth to include rhythmic heaving in the chest. Hal attempted to redirect his thoughts. He looked away, pondering the grandness, the beauty of the country. She was ageless—and implausibly pitiless. He was trying not to wallow in repulsion as he wiped the salty sweat from his face and labored in his duties for the rest of the afternoon. Still, at quitting time, it was hard to leave concerns and worries behind. One hardly dared wonder what tomorrow might bring.

The Japanese fleet *coincidently* moored itself directly across the river from the US fleet. Everyone knew they were spying on each other. Hal believed the "Japs" were too close for comfort, arrogant, unfriendly, and up to no good. It angered him that they were continually watching his navy through shaded binoculars. It was becoming more and more evident the Japs had no intention of leaving anytime soon. They behaved like they owned the place! Hal had his personal prejudices and suspicions. But he proudly wore patriotism on his sleeve. After all, he was part of a fully armed, invited fleet, and the Japs were imposing themselves where many knew they didn't belong. Nevertheless, both nesting navies rocked solidly in the surges of the Huangpu.

When the sun finally drooped seaward, Hal was thinking of home. He was glad to leave the ship, the sounds and smells of the day, and hurry home to the joy of his existence. Her name was Madelaine. She was the most beautiful, strong-willed woman Harold had ever met. But only time would reveal his underestimation of how wise and capable she was. He willed himself to think only of the sweetness, the tenderness they shared honeymooning in this mysterious land.

A sudden unexpected shiver raced down his spine. He was having second thoughts about bringing his bride to China. Was it the right thing to have done? He grinned, recalling her impulsive and cheeky voice. "Just try to stop me!" Oh yes, it was love at first sight that caused a rush to the altar with visions of sharing a beautiful future together— anywhere! By mutual agreement, life apart was no life at all.

Madelaine, of Swedish descent, was a blue-eyed, fair-skinned Oregonian. Adventuresome and robust, her coquettish smile radiated contentment and passion. In the style of the day, she finger-waved her silky blond hair, quietly humming, "Don't sit under the apple tree with anyone else but me, anyone else but me, anyone else but me ..." She was prettier than any movie star, and a bonus was her Betty Grable legs. Harold loved her softness and spunkiness and found joy merely thinking of her. Above all, he loved the way she loved him. Traces of violets, her scent, wafted through his mind. Oh yes, married life was magical, more exciting than any forever-after picture show. Mere thoughts of her gave him a feeling of added power and made troubles less significant.

He glanced at the coal shovels, carefully stowed, and wandered through the steel-gray passage to the deck. It was getting late, and the smells of a thousand busy woks drifted on the air, filling his nostrils with the aroma of zesty, Oriental chow. Hal was looking for a friend going his way. It suddenly occurred to the tired ole sea dog: he was famished.

The flat wasn't far off. First-rate luck, "Buddha luck," as Madelaine called it, found them a small upstairs flat not far from the ship. Hal could have walked home, but at the end of a hard day, he whistled for a rickshaw.

Cautious seamen were always on the watch for suspicious coolie behavior. It was best to walk or ride with a buddy, as dark alleyways teemed with danger. Personal safety was a significant issue. More than one tipsy seaman found himself rickshawed into a darkened alley, bloodied, and stripped of everything of value, including his life. The docks, eerily silent and lonely at dusk, reminded the wise to be extraordinarily cautious. But thoughts of sampans used for evil deeds were still haunting him. Hal did his best to stuff the terrible fervor aside and forced himself to think of home.

Down the narrow pier, surrounded by tired, white-capped sailors, Hal faced a sudden unruly mob of pushy capitalists. He realized selecting an honest rickshaw driver was becoming an artform. Spotting a redheaded shipmate, whose name he recalled as Sully, Hal motioned to him through the crowd.

Sully returned a curt nod, indicating that yes, he would appreciate being with a buddy, sharing a ride. They debated which Chinaman looked the most reliable and whistled to catch his attention. Hal pointed to the right, and the coolie nodded his head in agreement.

"Okay, Sully, get in. Let's take this one."

The men, emotionally and physically drained, were glad the day was over. Hal did his best to push unpleasant thoughts aside and replace them with images of his bride and their peaceful apartment. Sighing deeply, he was eager to get home, wash up, and shake off the blues. The nimble coolie hurried past crowds of people as the two men gabbed about the latest scuttlebutt and life in general. Narrow lanes became less crowded until only the sound of the clattering rickshaw was heard.

"Well, this is my stop," Hal finally said. Sully probably didn't hear his friend's parting words as the coolie sought final instructions.

"So long, pal. Keep your nose clean."

Hal trudged up the rickety staircase to the second floor and was welcomed with a dozen juicy kisses. Grinning seductively, Madelaine invited the handsome sailor to get comfortable in the humid flat. Not surprisingly, there was enough love and passion for him to ignore his growling stomach!

Late in the evening, Madelaine whispered, "There's a lot of prattle goin' on about a full-blown Jap invasion. If that were to happen, I might need a whole lot more of that first-rate luck getting outta here. You wouldn't sail away and leave me, would you?"

"Leave you? Never. But an emergency plan is always an excellent idea."

"I suppose we should talk about it—one of these days." Madelaine sighed.

"Yep." The sleepy sailor yawned. "I suppose we should. It's a good idea—one of these days."

While savvy intellectuals were whispering about the inevitability of war, Harold and others like him did their best to ignore the chatter. They were busily following orders and creating memories that would last forever. Thus, for the time being, the newlyweds pushed aside the opportunities for discussing cogent, viable emergency plans, should they ever be needed.

Delightfully, the following three years of ecstasy in China provided much more than Madelaine could ever have anticipated. "Harold was right," she whispered to herself. "Not at all what I expected."

CHAPTER 3

Yong Man—Big Suplize

Shanghai, China, 1939

From the window of their small apartment, Madelaine slowly moved the curtain aside and peered at the unfamiliar sights below. The street was noisy, filled with Oriental chatter and busy, busy, bustling crowds. She pinched herself for assurance; this was her new home. The long wait was finally over. Her sweetheart's arms and a new life on Liu Road were real. Yawning, she rubbed the sleep from her eyes and squinted at the noisy crowd. Was this the day Harold promised to Shanghai her for a rickshaw escapade in the city? Yes, yes, it was. But her man had been up early and mysteriously disappeared in the morning crowd. Before leaving, however, he whispered in her ear that he would return soon with "a big surprise."

In the market for a personal attendant for his lady, Harold hurried toward the river. He found Yong waiting for him on a dock near the ship. Yong was a shipshape Chinaman with excellent credentials—word of mouth from a chief shipping out. The smiling young soul seemed intelligent and responsible and advertised himself as an "honorable houseboy for hire." After a brief interview, the stranger shuffled obediently behind the grinning sailor. Yong's lengthy pigtail swayed quickly from side to side. Thin and grinning happily, he conversed in his own familiar brand of pidgin English.

Upon hearing noisy footsteps on the not-too-steady stairs leading to the upper landing, Madelaine opened the door to find two giddy men staring at her. One was her tall sailor, and the other, a foreigner of medium height—with a long black braid. Her eyes darted between the two of them as Harold kissed her cheek and introduced the cheery, respectful visitor.

"Meet Yong. He's gonna be your new best friend!"

She and Harold had talked about a houseboy—but for real? Wide-eyed, she looked at both men, cupped her mouth, and timidly whispered into Harold's ear, "Can we afford him?" Yong beamed brightly as the sailor's head bobbed affirmatively.

Grinning and pleased with himself, Hal whispered, "Vely good plice," and a firm handshake sealed the deal.

Skillful with a wok and scrubboard, Yong quickly became indispensable. He squatted on the floor and prepared authentic but less spicy meals for the sailorman and his lady. Yong was a master shopper, always finding the freshest fish and produce. He proudly taught his charges the fine art of managing sticky rice with a pair of chopsticks, though he preferred using a couple of fingers.

It also was Yong who selected rickshaws and coolies for Madelaine's outings. Waving his arms in the air, he lectured prospective drivers in the proper care of his charges, their absolute safety requirements, and other responsible coolie duties. When he was satisfied, Yong temporarily transferred responsibilities and worries to the thoroughly indoctrinated men. The English translation of Yong's instructions was something like "good safe lide and bring-ee home okey dokey." Madelaine smiled and volunteered that her own father hovered over and worried less about her than Yong. She often felt the need to say, "No, Yong, you don't have to go with us. I can carry my own packages, and I'll be perfectly fine."

Madelaine often talked of a cabinmate she met en route to the Orient aboard the *Tatura Maru*. Nina was a tall woman who identified herself as a white Russian. They shared a cabin and became good friends during the long, arduous trip.

Cultured and friendly, Nina spoke English with a thick, robust accent. From opposite sides of the world, the two women were surprised to have so much in common. Both were meeting their husbands in

Shanghai and experiencing their first visits to China. The ladies often met for afternoon outings and endless chatter. Both were adventuresome and enjoyed exploring unfamiliar places with a friend. Unfamiliar with the area and underestimating potential dangers, the friends unwittingly placed themselves at unnecessary risk because they lacked language skills or Oriental mindsets.

Nina was glad to have formed a keen friendship with Madelaine. "Ve learnt China togeder," Nina often said.

"Yagh, ve do," Madelaine replied, teasing her.

Nina was the wife of a wealthy merchant named Jacob. Their businesses were prospering, and plans were in the works for an ever-widening market. In contrast, Hal had little in common with the man—other than their wives' deepening friendship. Jacob was older than the sailor and highly respected in the business community. Fluent in several languages, he was a wizard in the world of finance. Besides their wives' friendship, the two men's principal interests were politics and mutual concerns over the widening influence of foreign powers.

"Are you at all alarmed about the way things are going?" Harold asked.

"Vell, yah, I tink about it," Jacob answered. Quickly changing the subject, Jacob smiled and said, "Kum overt to da factory vone of dees days, Harolt, unt I show you arount."

While their wives explored "safe, secure" sections of the city, highly recommended by Yong, of course, the four friends simply speculated about current and future events and chatted over tea. What did a bunch of foreigners really know of politics or the internal affairs of bickering nations? Just a nagging feeling, one might suppose.

CHAPTER 4

Settlin' on the Liu

Shanghai, China, 1939

When Madelaine wasn't shopping, receiving culinary lessons from Yong, or meeting with friends, she wrote copious letters. Her fountain pen, full of coffee-brown ink, was never at a loss for words. A writer at heart, she composed her thoughts on onionskin paper and checked her little black book for addresses and stamps. She kept a journal of bright ideas, hopes, aspirations—and original poetry. Harold significantly cherished a verse she posted to him shortly after his deployment. It read:

"To My Heart"
Beat slowly, oh my troubled heart.
Cease thy pounding pace
That I may greet my lover
With a calm and smiling face.

Harold kept all of her letters; he read and reread them. It thrilled him to know how much he was loved. His heart had been an empty glass, but she filled it over and over with love, security, and joy. How could he ever discard her precious, written thoughts?

Madelaine opened a bureau drawer and discovered delicate envelopes addressed to him in her own handwriting. The lightweight letters were mailed from San Francisco, written only months before she sailed. Removing a random envelope, she relived the memories and the feelings as she read:

> My dearest, darling husband, I can hardly wait to hold you in my arms. Our separation has been unbearable, and I dream of little else but being with you again. We finally have enough money for a one-way, third-class ticket, which I'm holding next to my heart. The travel agent tried to convince me to buy a round-trip ticket, but we only have enough money to travel one way. Do you suppose you could hide me in your seabags if I needed to get home on the double? We'll jest about that later. My ship sails from San Francisco on the fifteenth of next month, and I'm too excited to do much else but dream of you, of us. I don't have much to pack, and I only have one little suitcase. I was fortunate to secure a ticket on the Japanese luxury liner, the *Tatura Maru*. To help you recognize me, I'll be wearing a blue knitted dress and waving like a madwoman—me, the bride who refuses to live without you, breathless and passionately anticipating our wonderful future.

She smiled, folded the crisp, thin paper, and replaced the letter in its envelope. It was easy to recall the few months they'd shared before the difficult separation. Thoughts of loneliness were easy to remember, and the emptiness she once felt. The ink was hardly dry on the marriage certificate before the navy sent Harold to the Orient. If she, an Oregonian, thought San Francisco was exhilarating, he promised China would knock her socks off.

"I'll find a place for us," Harold vowed. "Someday, we'll get back to unfinished business, a honeymoon we'll never forget."

But, it was so painful watching the stately gray ship sail under the Golden Gate, leaving her alone on the dock. She wished it had only been the fog that wetted her soul, but it was not.

Madelaine immediately scoured the *Chronicle*, looking for work, and quickly found a job as a waitress at a prestigious country club overlooking the sea. Her pleasing figure and witty personality made her very popular. She winked, charmed the elite, and collected generous tips. Hustling on weekends and holidays, she worked overtime at every opportunity.

The cash quickly fattened the honeymoon fund, and when she'd saved just enough money for a slow boat to China, she fumbled with certified tickets and gushed with excitement. Though she was now settling into her new life, she always recalled the thrill of the *Tatura Maru* being underway. A Japanese luxury liner, the ship promised adventure, newness, and endless passion halfway around the world.

When the stately steamer docked in China, the sight of his bride took Harold's breath away. Gesturing wildly, she ran to him, carrying only a small tan suitcase and deep pockets overflowing with joy. Swimming in the blue of her eyes, Hal whispered that even life in heaven would be miserable without her. Then he grinned broadly. "Let's go home, honey, and get down to brass tacks—to the honeymoon we've been missin'. Wait 'til you see the place I found!"

It was adequate, a comfortable nest for a pair of lovebirds in a somewhat secure section of the city. Of course, China had its own definition of safe and secure. Adjusting to new living ways came fairly quickly, especially when Yong became a hardworking household member.

One bright morning, Madelaine was distracted by quick footsteps on the landing. With morning chores behind him and a spiffy Chinaman in tow, Harold was a sailor in a hurry. Yong paced conspicuously, trying to communicate his concerns. Though he'd been chitchatting with Harold all morning, nobody seemed to be paying attention to him or even listening. Yong had important news nobody wanted to hear.

"We got plenty to see today," Harold said. "What's takin' ya so long?"

"I'll be ready in a few," Madelaine called.

Her short yellow curls bounced as she primped. Grinning, she sported the latest style, a permanent hair wave. Humming, she applied another coat of red lipstick, smiled, and admired the pixy in the mirror.

Youthful, she was often mistaken for a teenager. But her passport was a giveaway: "American citizen, age twenty-seven, 5' tall (in heels)."

Satisfied with her comely appearance, she inspected the buttons on her summer blouse, confident they were correctly fastened. Then she unbuttoned the top to reveal a hint of coquettishness. Straightening her floral skirt, she smiled approvingly. The soft pink of it complemented her femininity.

"He'll notice," she calculated.

At last, Madelaine spoke over her shoulder. "I'm ready, honey." She tucked a clean white handkerchief in a small clutch and turned to leave.

Yong was pacing again.

"Don't worry about us! You worry too much. We'll be just fine," said Madelaine.

The frustrated houseboy upshifted the pitch of his voice. But preoccupied, the couple neither saw nor heard a thing but noise. In desperation, Yong switched to singsong Chinese and said he could read the weather. The clouds were too heavy for sightseeing. A storm was brewing. But no amount of persuasion put off the lovers. The more animated the servant became, the less English he remembered. Finally, in total frustration, he wigwagged his arm in the air and jabbered at top speed.

When the door slammed shut, Yong stood alone, ignored in the quiet room. Undeterred, he shrugged his shoulders and continued a conversation with himself. Heaving resolutely, he scooped up a couple of large wicker baskets, shook his head, and headed to the marketplace.

"'Melican sailor, no hear," he mumbled. Nervously, still hoping to be understood, he opened the door and stepped onto the high, narrow porch. The laughing couple was descending the staircase at a dangerous clip.

"Look-see, muchee no good. No go—no good time. No walk-ee so fast!" Yong leaned over the loose railing and added, "Old stair no safe. Need slow walk-ee time."

Harold squinted from the lane below and pointed upward. The sky was crystal blue, except for a few puffy clouds drifting aimlessly. Turning to Yong, Hal responded, "You been sippin' too muchee rice juice!"

Turning deaf ears to the red-faced man, the lovers raced to the main road, waving goodbye. Tuned only into themselves, they were a couple of kids in love. Out of Yong's sight, Madelaine doubled over with laughter. She mimicked the houseboy's gestures, confident the inflection in her voice—the dialect she used—was his. And, crazy in love, she mercilessly teased the laughing sailor.

"Come on, you. We got muchee good times ahead—unless you have other plans …"

CHAPTER 5

Garden of Delights

Newlyweds Exploring Chinese Culture, 1939

The eager lovers waved to a somber coolie pulling a colorful rickshaw from the side of a shadeless road. Sensing an easy fare, the thin man motioned for the couple to hop in. Harold attempted to haggle with the stranger in clipped Oriental English. And in frustration, they finally pointed to a spot on a well-worn map. Hal said they wanted "Chop-chop ride—little yuan! No shortcuts, no funny business! Stay on the main road to the Yuyuan Gardens.[1] You know?"

"Yeah, yeah, yeah," replied the nodding coolie.

Satisfied, Harold gestured to Madelaine and said, "Hop in, hon. He knows the way."

A tightly woven umbrella covered the rickshaw, promising relief from the heat of the sun. It lied. Some distance into the ride, the sailor squirmed uncomfortably. Leaning forward and trying to catch the coolie's attention, he asked, "How far, Yu?"

"Not vely," Madelaine quipped as she studied the map. She smiled and measured the distances with her fingers. "About an inch," she added. "The air is so unbearably humid." She sighed. "I'm *so* hot!"

Hal grinned. "Shall we double back to the apartment?"

Kissing him passionately, she whispered, "Yu first."

---

[1] The Garden of Contentment, established in 1559.

Despite the weather, the ride was a feast of unusual, exhilarating sights and smells. Madelaine's cotton skirt hung limply over her shapely legs. Provocatively, she fanned herself with a corner of the fabric.

"Whew," she said. "I could use a little puff of air. Even a wisp would do."

Hal was about to offer his services when the rickshaw slowed for traffic. Suddenly an oasis of beauty loomed ahead.

"Look!" Madelaine exclaimed. "This has to be the place."

Staring in rapt attention, Hal ordered the driver to follow the well-manicured pathway, hoping the leafy wonders would bring relief from the blazing sun. He needn't have given the order, as the rickshaw was already veering left.

"Stop here," Hal finally said to the red-faced driver.

Peeling themselves from the cramped seat, he handed the coolie a couple of yuan, including a generous tip. Then bowing politely, Hal told the driver he was free to go.

Breathing heavily, the man replied, "No Engrish! No talk-ee Engrish!"

Hal blushed, and Madelaine snickered.

"Thanks again. Vely nice ride. Don't wait, we okay," Madelaine said to the driver, brushing him away.

"*No* Engrish!" he scowled.

"I feel so darn silly." Hal chuckled. "Been talkin' to myself the entire way!"

Swiping his face again, the coolie merged into heavy traffic. As he did, he turned and offered a toothless grin, knowing the sailor man and his lady were hot, happy 'Melicans, or something akin to it.

Madelaine waved and added, "Shay-shay."

An official paper firmly attached to a post at the garden entrance noted ordinary Chinese citizens were forbidden to enter.

"Them Japs are makin' things miserable for everyone," Harold grumbled. "Before they took over, this place was a national treasure. It once belonged to a prominent Chinese family, and they decided who was welcome and who was not. This historic place has been part of Chinese culture for centuries, the pamphlet said." Hal added, "At least them foreigners ain't done nothin' to destroy it—yet."

The place was a photographer's dream as a silent army of Chinese gardeners snipped and trimmed. However, Hal and Madelaine took little notice of anyone but themselves and the peace that enfolded them as they strolled amid the exotic, pungent foliage. Nostrils filled with the exquisite scents of roses, gardenias, sweet peas, and other species of flora lining the meandering paths. It was a mélange of color, though the verdant, ancient trees were eerily still.

Harold noted the drifting clouds seemed to be conspicuously gathering, a sure promise of more massive humidity. "Perhaps we should be thinking of getting home before we're drenched," Madelaine said. "I'm smelling rain in the air, and I wonder if Yong was predicting another one of those sudden summer rainstorms."

"Maybe." Hal smiled." Let's hail another driver and head for Lui Road. We could use a little rest ... and I have plenty of other things on my mind!"

CHAPTER 6

Lovin' Lui

Honeymooning in the China Rain, 1940

"I'll help with those bundles," Harold volunteered as a sudden squall pulled at the treasures in Madelaine's arms.

Her platinum curls danced uneasily. Leaning into Hal's chest, she said, "There's a storm brewing. The city's much cooler, but I think it's time to hurry home. We've shopped enough for today."

"Sky, no lookie good. We go click," said the hired coolie.

"He's serious, honey. Yong might be right about those clouds. I smell the rain, and the sky's apt to leak on us before we find shelter," Madelaine said.

"Nobody can smell the rain," Hal teased. "It ain't nothin' but water."

"Oregonians can smell rain ten miles away," she replied, "and I smell it!"

Harold rolled his eyes. "Okey dokey, if you say so. Driver, on the double. Chop-chop pronto."

The rickshaw picked up speed as it rushed past tired ancient gray houses. Generations of the families occupied the dwellings, each shack with bamboo rods protruding from upper-story windows.

"Is that the Chinese version of a clothesline?" Madelaine queried.

"Yep," Harold said. "You see 'em all over China. When we were in windy Tsingtao, sometimes I wondered what held 'em in place. They reminded me of flagpoles with flappin' wet rags tryin' to get loose. It's the norm."

Above the rickshaw, dingy long johns appeared agitated as busy hands, sensing the worst, reeled them in.

"Someday, I'm gonna write a poem about those fluttering undies," Madelaine mused. Good at it, she liked to compose and amused herself with poetry scribbled in her little black book.

"A poem about underwear?" Harold snickered. "Lemme hear it. I'm waitin'. This oughta be good!"

"Well," replied Madelaine, "it'll go something like this …" Smiling, she began to recite. "I'll call it:

> 'Sad but True'
> (Because it is!)
> They were gray with age and badly worn.
> The legs were patched where they were torn.
> But that was not the reason why
> I noticed them as I passed by.
> Not the patches on that underwear
> But the hopeless way they flapped up there.
> They seemed to have so little pride
> As they limply hung there on the line.
> That cold, wet, gray underwear
> That once was white and fine!"

With poetic license, Harold roared, "You are *so* funny, honey." The couple laughed and pointed to more sets of long johns undulating in the air. They seemed to be instigating hostilities toward headless garments on adjacent lines. Madelaine squealed with girlish delight as the blustery wind curled and snapped at loaded, unattended poles.

A sudden clap of thunder raddled the air as heavy clouds pelted the gray-tiled roofs. Torrential downpours weren't uncommon, but Harold hoped this would be a quick one. Too late, the driver scurried for shelter. Water gushed onto the pavement, reminding one of a public bathhouse. Shrill, rapid chatter did little to abate conditions as agitated merchants hustled to gather their wares. Midair, Harold snatched the daily rag. It hinted of an offer of protection from the deluge, but the *China Press* did little to keep anybody dry as an impromptu umbrella. Pedestrians and drowning rats scurried for safety as the wheels of the rickshaw chattered through the crowded street.

"Look," Madelaine whispered. "The coolie's bamboo hat resembles an inverted funnel." Useless, it drenched him from head to toe. Heartlessly, the rain careened down his hunched back, into his trousers and sandals. By the time the buggy turned onto Liu Road, the cloudburst and thunder clapped all the more threateningly.

"Just a bit farther!" Hal yelled. "Oh! I see it. Pull to the left. We're here."

Hal helped Madelaine from the coach and eagerly handed off to the driver several soggy yuan. Sheltering her eyes, Madelaine called, "Thank you," but he didn't respond. He leaned into the storm and hurried away, clearly preoccupied with more important matters. The couple, clutching their purchases, bolted toward the glassy staircase. The sailor sheltered his tiny wife and prized acquisitions with his tall, youthful body.

"You're especially beautiful soaked to the bone," he said, grinning.

She looked at him, pushed a droopy lock from her eyes, and smiled. "Am I?"

He passionately held her and kissed her under the useless newspaper.

"Let's get upstairs—and out of these waterlogged duds."

"I can hardly wait," she said.

Amused and hopelessly in love, the couple sprinted up the steep wooden stairway. The never-ending hubbub momentarily dulled as Harold fumbled with the slippery key. He said they couldn't get any wetter than they already were. Saving him the bother, Yong swung the door wide open and greeted his charges with a couple of dry bath towels and a frown. Full bore, he rambled about unheeded warnings, waiting impatiently, worrying, and fretting for the safety of his charges.

"Missy, Sailorman vely wet. Maybe slippy fall. Lost, hungry. No lice, no tea. I worry!" Pointing heavenward, he continued, "Big lain vely noisy on loof, but no leakee ..." Not even summer storms interfered with his dutiful responsibilities. After his high-pitched say-so, Yong passed the inattentive, preoccupied lovers on the landing and sheepishly excused himself.

"I—uh—vely glad you OK. I here tomollow."

Yong was especially cautious as he descended the slippery stairs. He held tightly to the wobbly banister, muttering something about "fixee sumday." Holding his useless bamboo umbrella, he disappeared, not bothering to look back. The soggy lovebirds closed the door, grateful to be alone in the quiet, peaceful room. The sweet smell of orange blossom tea was pungent. Harold supposed Yong had it ready, knowing his charges would be wet and cold.

"Here, put this cloth around your wet head," Hal said, "and let's slip into those new silky robes we just bought."

"You may get more than you bargained for." The bride grinned as she looked deeply into his beautiful brown eyes, moist with love.

"I hope so," he whispered. "I sure hope so …"

The music of the rain was hypnotic, inviting sweetness and passion. They say Shanghai was awash with beautiful reflections on that sultry night, prettier than a picture postcard—but then, who noticed?

CHAPTER 7

Chi-Foo-Sung

Chinese Adventures, Opera

"My snoz is tellin' me we're close to chow," the sailor said.

"Me too," Madelaine replied. "It's been a busy day."

Just ahead, alluring aromas wafted through the open doors as a bevy of friendly waiters hustled would-be diners into the crowded restaurant. Fortunately, the sidewalk crowd was thinning abruptly as kowtowing waiters welcomed business, shoving well-used menus at hungry customers.

"Juicy Peking duck? Nice flesh—you choose. I fixee you, chop-chop. Come in. Come in," the waiter beckoned.

Eager for business, the toothy boss man smiled broadly. Colorful menus said it all: fast woks, good food, and low prices. The eatery lacked space, but the smells of Asian spices flowing from the kitchen made up for any perceived deficiencies. Harold's mouth watered.

"We serve best flied lice in Shanghai," the waiter promised. "Nice table for 'Melicans. You sit here. I bringee vely, vely good food. Entertain in half-owe-ah. You like opera, yes, yes? We have vely, v-e-l-y famous Chinese opera."

Before Harold could say no, the headman clapped his hands, and the starving foreigners became the center of attention. Noisy waiters jabbered in high-pitched tones as they busily carried trays of steaming morsels. The aroma of oily noodles, vegetable dishes, and a multitude of unknowns wafted through the air. Madelaine drooled at plates piled high with luscious concoctions. She was certain two of them were meant for their table. Craning her neck for a better view, her head bobbed in rhythm with the hectic, oblivious waitstaff.

Harold hadn't finished his dinner when several ornately dressed sopranos, famous singers of ancient Chinese operas, screeched and floated onto a make-do stage. Nothing sounded as foreign to the jitterbuggers as clanging cymbals, overactive, painted drummers, and the bowing of three-stringed instruments. Madelaine felt her mouth drop as the piercing and uncomfortable sounds fell on unappreciative ears. She'd always enjoyed opera, she thought. In the States, she often listened to the music coming from the Met. China, however, was not home! High-pitched and irksome, the music seemed endless and far too loud for comfort.

Knowing the certainty of Harold's reply, Madelaine cupped her hands, funneling her mouth, and said over the bedlam, "You likee opera?"

"No!"

Gongs and chimes sounding in rapid succession invited the performers to shuffle even closer to the patrons.

"Good grief!" Harold said. "There must be a five-alarm fire going on. Let's find some boxes for the grub and get outta here. This racket's killin' my ears. Besides, I have better ideas for the evening's entertainment."

Evening? Madelaine glanced at her watch. It was only late afternoon. Her soft blue eyes flashed in rhythm with his.

"Chop-chop," she replied. "I'm hurrying!"

To the grinning waiter, she said, "We take v-e-l-y fine carry-out food home. No more opera! Husband very tired. Sensitive 'Melican ears!"

"V-e-l-y famous," the attendant boasted.

Madelaine nodded, bowed politely, and slid carefully between the busy staff to the front door. Harold did his best to protect his ears and followed her with an armful of boxes.

"You come tomorrow? More big opera ..."

Of course, neither a rickshaw nor taxi was anywhere in sight when most desperately needed!

"Let's just follow the main road. More and more of these old buildings are looking familiar. I think we can find our way home," said Harold. "The after-dinner walk will do us good. My ears are still ringing!"

Strolling on cobblestone streets wasn't a new experience. Block after persistent block, aggressive vendors along the way did their best to entice the curious. The guide book said Nanjing Road was the place to shop.

Since her arrival in the Orient, Madelaine had been intrigued by the game of mahjong. She watched people gather in parks, laughing and concentrating as they moved game pieces in various directions. Someday she'd learn to play, she hoped. Nina played, and so did Yong.

"Come see. You like, you buy! I makee vely good plice."

The shop also sold beautiful jade statuary. Genuine jade, the vendor volunteered, can always be identified, as it is always cold to the touch. His carvings were irresistible, very cold, and delicate. The vendor also supplied intricately carved dragons, round-bellied Buddhas of solid, polished wood, and others made of exquisitely carved jade. Harold noted the handcrafted, identical tiny ivory teeth that graced Buddha's perpetually happy smile.

"Walkee 'round Buddha three times. Lub belly like this," the smiling Chinaman demonstrated. "Laughing Buddha always grant every wish come true."

Madelaine did her best to stifle a giggle. The resemblance between the vendor and his goods was remarkable.

"Here," said Harold, handing the massive carving to his wife. "This big one is going home with us. We could use more belly-lubbing and laughin' luck. Buddha, meet new sailor family. All speakee vely good Engrish."

Madelaine laughed at his silly imitations and admired the superb quality of the objects. Bowing, she thanked the vendor as he wrapped her purchases with yesterday's newspaper and carefully placed them in a large, colorful sack.

Steps away, a thin, shy man timidly said, "Lady need pearl cleam?

Vely nice for soft white skin. I give good plice, m-o-s-t soft," he promised. And it was. Into the shopping bag went the small bottle of expensive cream. It was the best cream in the world!

Continuing their stroll toward home, Madelaine spied tables of needle handiwork. "Beautiful, beautiful," she said. The pieces were hand embroidered works of art. She examined the silken threads. The artistry was flawless—floral patterns, seascapes, koi fish swimming lazily in invisible ponds, landscapes hand sewn on raw silk and linen.

"Look," she cooed. "This is a must—and this—and this. These pieces will make wonderful gifts. Look at the back of this embroidery. The quality is dazzling."

Marveling at the hankies she held in her hands, Madelaine commented that no one in the States would believe how cheap the beautiful pieces were. "I should buy more and put them away ..."

Yards and yards of shantung silk and brocades trailed from the arms of a smiling seller. The fabric flowed as effortlessly as liquid silver. Softer than rose petals, it glistened from dozens of enticing bolts stored overhead and shelves surrounding the crowded shop's parameter. Delicate hues of turquoise, emerald, gold, scarlet, snowy white—they were gorgeous—shimmering seductively in the sunlight.

Confident he'd found a winner, Harold bargained like a native. And at last, satisfied with his bargaining skills, he handed the rewards to his wife. Grinning, Harold added a silk dress, slip, and intricately embroidered, matching robes.

"Someday, these beautiful things will go into our own home. When we look at them, we'll remember this place, this day, these feelings, and the good, hardworking people who created and sold them," she said.

"Do you think we'll ever have a home of our own?" Harold queried.

"Oh yes, and a couple of kids." She grinned. "Maybe we'll even have a white picket fence." That thought was beyond Harold's comprehension!

Changing the subject, she said, "These packages and boxes are getting heavy."

"We should have bought more. These treasures are dirt cheap," Harold said. "But I think it's high time to find a rickshaw." His inspiration came from swollen feet, arms full of massive purchases, and the unmistakable sound of an empty buggy turning the corner.

"Aah," said the ladened bride. "Just what the doctor ordered."

The couple, with laps full of treasures, enjoyed a close ride. Fortunately, a light breeze made the heat less oppressive. Carefully dodging carriages, cars, and pedestrians, the nimble driver hurried abreast of the Huangpu. His fee was the final one of the day.

"Only short way more," promised the coolie. "Chop-chop."

CHAPTER 8

Made in China

China Amid Brewing Storm Clouds, April 1940

For nearly three years, Tsingtao's ancient city and the bustling city of Shanghai provided unusual and exciting quarters for a pair of naive honeymooners, thanks to the United States Navy. When the ship moved, Madelaine and Yong followed. In the evenings, Harold rushed home for more rice and another helping of love.

It was dinnertime when Hal carelessly reached across the table for another slippery, flavorful mushroom. He popped it into his mouth and rolled his eyes in appreciation.

"Mmm," he mumbled. "You sure can cook, Yong! This here food is larrupin' good stuff." Nearly a pro with his chopsticks, he moved them like miniature stilts as Madelaine watched the rice disappear from his bowl.

"And another excitin' thing about the *Augusta*, she's the admiral's flagship," Hal said as he reached for more oily noodles. "The admiral's flag waving means plenty." Moored safely in the deep, busy river, the USS *Augusta* (CA-31) was a fine-looking warship, and Harold was proud of her. His rhetoric didn't mean much to his under-the-weather wife at the moment—but it soon would.

Suddenly, she interrupted his navy babbling.

"Honey, I'm not feeling very well. If you don't mind, I'm gonna rest and see if my stomach settles down. I'm feeling greener than those Gravensteins. Maybe I have been eating too many, but I can't seem to get enough."

Hal quickly finished his meal and did his best to attend to her needs. Her unhealthy demeanor was uncharacteristically listless and somber. Hal had been taking note of his wife's frequent tabletop stares and extreme drowsiness. Frankly, it was disconcerting. She was about to say something but suddenly rolled her eyes and frantically dashed to the honeypot—which was neither fit for honey nor comforting to the stomach. Harold looked at her with sympathy written all over his face. "Here's some fresh water and a cool cloth. I hope it helps." It was a thoughtful gesture, but it was not at all helpful!

Madelaine didn't reply. She was too busy hovering over the honeypot. With deep concern, Hal frowned again. "Honey, I think you need to see one of them navy doctors on the double."

Helpless to remedy the situation, he kissed her on the forehead and helped her recline on several fluffy cushions. Then, turning his attention to Yong, Hal noted the houseboy also had an air of empathetic unwellness. Ill-timed as it was, Hal proceeded with his tender thoughts.

"Yong, I appreciate you takin' such good care of Madelaine and me, keeping her steady an' safe an', well—calm, 'specially when I'm at sea. You're a good man, and we both want you to know having you with us, well, we're truly grateful for your help. I, uh, we truly 'preciate all you do. You're an awful good man."

Yong blushed and bowed his head respectfully. "You, Missy, good 'Melicans. I take vely, vely good care of the little wife. Number one houseboy; good plice, v-e-r-y good service." He grinned. The Orient was a place where even a little dough from a sailor meant something. And Yong, Hal concluded, was their finest outlay.

Per instructions, Yong did his best to keep Madelaine calm and rested. When she craved more fresh fruit, he rode his bike far into the countryside to find the apple she described—not just any apple; only Gravensteins would do. The green-skinned fruit was crisp and juicy, and unfortunately, her appetite was insatiable. She couldn't help herself. She ate baskets of them and nauseously ran for the honeypot—again. She wondered if she might have picked up a bug from too hastily washing the fruit or eating so much of it at a time. But the tangy cravings weren't subsiding, and her complexion was beginning to match the apples. Teasingly, Harold said she had mastered the green-apple-quick-step!

Yong said they needed to take extra care with the drinking water. Perhaps the cause of her illness was something swimming in the water bucket, or maybe something left by the enormous rats that were seldom inconvenienced by humans. Madelaine promised she'd visit the dispensary soon and hoped some little pill or a tablespoon of anything would ease her problems.

"Mrs. Foltz," said the doctor, "congratulations. We're certain you're pregnant. But you're losing too much weight, 94.7 pounds, and dropping. I'm concerned about your continual weight loss. And I'm certain what you are experiencing is round-the-clock morning sickness. My advice is to drink plenty of fluids and rest as much as possible. It might be helpful to keep some plain broth in your stomach—and a few crackers. Eat light portions often, and call me if nausea persists."

Thinking aloud, she muttered, "Nothin' could be worse than this. Just the smell, the thought of food makes me gag!"

Smiling, the doctor wisely suggested, "You might want to decrease the consumption of so much fruit." He looked up from scribbling on a pad of paper and said, "I'd like to see you in a week, or sooner if the vomiting increases." She was about to speak when she suddenly reached for a nearby basin and threw up even before leaving the room!

"A what?" Harold exclaimed. "You mean I'm gonna be a father? Oh, hon, that's wonderful. We're gonna have a baby! It's about time we start lookin' into getting you back to the States real soon if we want our baby born on American soil." He wanted to hug her, but she settled for a light kiss on the cheek—and hurried to the honeypot again.

Yong became the Chinese version of a mother hen. "Missy, rest now. Missy, no shoppy. Missy, slow eat Grabunzeins. Makey face green. Missy sippy light fish juice soup …"

In the heat of the summer of 1940, notes and letters from Madelaine's pen filled with coffee-brown ink revealed the inevitable. Her overexcited handwriting announced to friends and family she was expecting a baby sometime in late January or early February. She spoke of morning sickness that lasted morning, noon, and night, of the delicious apples, and Yong's devoted attention. She added that the souvenir she planned to bring home would be a permanent reminder of their blissful honeymoon in the Orient.

On good days, the trio tried their best to ignore the endless chitchat of escalating troubles in the world, most notably with Japan. Perhaps the presence of the finest navy in the world should have provided a sense of security. But war clouds grew thicker, darker. Naively, many people did their best to look the other way, hoping reports of developing worldwide sicknesses were erroneous. Neither Harold, Madelaine, nor Yong wanted to acknowledge the ugliness and dangers of impending warfare, but the apparent truth loomed menacingly close, just beyond the rising sun.

CHAPTER 9

Only Time Will Tell

Accidents never happen at convenient times!

Shanghai, November 1940

"I'll be out of your way all day, Yong. My Russian friend invited me to her place for lunch. She's gonna teach me to play mahjong. Did we show you the beautiful, hand-carved set we bought? Neither Harold nor I have a clue how to play the game. We've watched so many other people laughing and playing; it's about time we find a master teacher while we're still here in China. Don't worry about a thing, Yong. I'm feeling reasonably well today. Nina's sending a car for me, and I'm pretty confident it will take a long time to learn the rules of the game. You just enjoy yourself and don't worry about anything. Harold has the duty, but we'll both be home for dinner. I'm leaving some yuan on the table for you. I think you said you wanted to go to the marketplace this afternoon. Would you mind buying a couple of greenie Gravensteins if they have any?" Usually, Yong pedaled his bike far into the countryside to find the only apple that appeased her longing.

Madelaine was gathering a few last-minute items, rushing to be ready when the car arrived. She hoped her nonstop chatter would not give Yong any leeway for reasonable backtalk. He was always worrying about her safety and not at all convinced she was well enough to be out all day.

"What if—" he started.

"Oh, there's the car, Yong," she quickly interrupted. "Take a little time for yourself this afternoon, and don't work too hard. I smell rain comin', so I'm takin' the umbrella."

Grateful to have the dreadful morning sickness mostly under control, she scrupulously followed the doctor's orders and swallowed gallons of pink antinausea medicine.

Ducking carefully out the door, she waved to Yong and Nina's waiting driver. For once, Madelaine wasn't charging down the stairs—not feeling all that steady. But the shakiness seemed more pronounced than usual. Was it her or the tired old railing?

Madelaine had good news to share with her friends and anticipated a fun-filled afternoon with Nina, her former cabinmate. True to form, they laughed and reminisced about experiences on the long cruise aboard the *Tatura Maru*. San Francisco and home didn't seem so far away as the ladies recalled memories of family hugs and best wishes on that rainy, foggy morning with family members standing on the dock. "Au voir!" Nina's family shouted. The long ocean voyage turned strangers into best friends. Both were settling into new lives and Oriental routines.

Nina's experienced driver was traveling slowly and cautiously on the busy streets. He was sharing space with hundreds of bicyclists, pedestrians, and rickshaws.

"Be careful!" Madelaine lectured the professional chauffeur. Unsmiling, he stared into the rearview mirror at her and said nothing. She understood the implicit message and did her best not to cringe at the daring riders pedaling only inches from the car's windows—young mothers with toddlers strapped to their backs, a baby in the arms of a woman on a rusty old bicycle built for two, and peddlers carefully making their way through the insane traffic.

Nina's home was in an unfamiliar part of town. The fenced-in mansions and manicured yards were breathtakingly lovely. Madelaine thought she might have been in an exclusive part of Europe with maids and butlers eager to serve—not the raucous city of Shanghai with its distractions and tension. Unlike her own, Nina's neighborhood was quiet and peaceful.

"Wow, this is more like it!" Madelaine whispered to herself.

The chauffeur slowed as he reached the gate of a beautiful Victorian home. *This must be the place*, she thought. And, indeed, it was. Nina was waiting comfortably on a wraparound veranda as the driver ushered his charge to the front steps.

"Oh, Nina, this place is stunning!"

"Vel," she said, grinning, "Yacob done vell buildink our business. Ven Harolt retiret vrom da navy, der might ve vroom for hem en da company. Ve growink so fast. Ve alvays neet good hep."

"What an interesting thought, Nina. But with world events changing so quickly, we may need all the more navy men we can find. Do you suppose Jacob would be interested in a little nautical interlude? I'll bet he'd be useful in redesigning those handsome navy uniforms for the heat of the Orient! We'd put in a good word for ya."

The two friends were about to settle down for a long-awaited mahjong lesson. They admired the ivory game pieces. Real ivory? Yes, they were—at a terrible cost to the animals producing it. Intricately hand-carved works were all too plentiful in the marketplace. Nina suggested a stroll onto the grounds, touring her well-manicured, peaceful garden. It was a radical change from everyday life on the Liu. Nina's world almost seemed out of place from the busy, noisy world Madelaine knew, a world of chaos and turmoil.

"Are you and Jacob concerned at all about a full-out Jap invasion? Do you have any contingency plans should an evacuation be necessary? Do you worry about your home being invaded or the business being confiscated?"

"Neit, neit—ve secure. Ve not vorry. But ve vould go back to da States, if necessary." She then gave Madelaine a sideways glance. Madelaine tried to feel secure, but she was definitely a long way from home with no concrete plans for their uncertain future. Even if she did have a plan, there was no money with which to fund it.

"Well, Harold and I will settle down and talk about it really soon," she replied. "It only makes sense. Everyone needs to have alternative plans, especially with a baby on the way."

Nina was happy for her friend. She and Jacob had been too busy building their highly successful businesses, and there didn't seem to be room in their lives for children. "Da vorlt is too angry, too unstablt vor families nowadays. Ve stay vit silk unt vools.

"Ve play mahjong now," Nina suddenly said, changing the subject and steering them toward the house. "Ve got rules unt plays to learnt."

Yong noted the stairs to the sailorman's flat seemed to be creaking more than usual. The old wood shook as he carried baskets of groceries to the upstairs unit. "I bringee sailorman look-see," he thought aloud.

At the end of his shopping day, and incredibly uncomfortable, Yong hauled several more baskets of supplies to the apartment. The railing seemed more fragile, shakier, less supportive than usual. He felt anxious, though he wasn't sure why. A sudden thought filled his mind. What if Missy misstepped, or the railing gave way on its own? He'd always known it needed a carpenter's attention, but no one was making any effort to repair anything.

The stairs were old and tired of supporting a multitude of tenants. Who knew how many decades the building had been standing? Chipped paint and splinters attested to years of heavy traffic. No one remembered who built it or when. But it was apparent to Yong that it needed maintenance. Unfortunately, it was the shaky stairs that provided the only access to the flat. Yong had climbed it hundreds of times and was confident someone should have replaced or repaired the rickety stairs years ago. The usefulness of the railing had also long since vanished. It was supposed to add a measure of security but didn't. It took a great deal of imagination to think the stairs had once been well built, pridefully painted, and fastened securely. Like a detective, Yong began to notice many nails were missing, and the few remaining were rusty from years of weathering and stress. He intended to bring the matter to the sailorman's attention that very evening.

Yong had been warning the young couple to be cautious, but they seemed to make a game of running up and down the unstable boards, ignoring the movement and splintered railing. Someone was going to get hurt. He knew it for sure. Perhaps, he thought, it was merely an unwanted premonition.

By late afternoon, Yong was even more concerned about his charges. When did she say she'd be home? The sailor should already have been there, but for some reason, he too was late. Then suddenly, Yong heard a commotion from the street below. By the time he recognized familiar voices, the driver had already slammed the car door and was on his way home. Madelaine was already climbing the stairs.

Yong rushed to the unsteady porch when he heard the crash. She'd supported her weight on the unstable railing, and it suddenly gave way, sending her tumbling to the ground. It was a terrible accident, and a crowd of onlookers was already gathering as Yong sprinted to the street.

"Missy! Missy!" he hollered, but there was no response. She was unconscious.

Harold was just turning the corner when he saw the crowd. Yong screamed in horror, terrified and hysterical. Dashing to the ghastly sight, Hal knelt beside her body, too shocked to think straight. He'd never seen an unconscious person, and there she was—his pregnant wife, still and bleeding. Was she breathing?

"Ambulance come, chop-chop," volunteered a stranger.

"It's going to take a while to know the extent of the damage," the doctor explained. "We're going to keep her in the hospital, take some more tests, and wait. Let's hope for the best and see what tomorrow brings."

It was far more comforting for Madelaine to sleep than to absorb the shock of seeing the damage she'd sustained. The left side of her face drooped hideously. She suffered a head injury that caused paralysis to the left side of her body. Was it going to be permanent? How would it affect the rest of her young life? "Only time will tell, Mrs. Foltz."

"What about my baby? Will we be all right?"

The doctor sighed heavily and reluctantly repeated his encouraging words: "Only time will tell."

CHAPTER 10

Nightmares and Prayers

China, 1949

For centuries, folklore claimed that honorable, spiritual dragons protected China's shores. But neighboring armies were aggressively lusting for all the vast, beautiful lands as well as the natural resources of her ancient fathers. As the buildup of foreign warships increased, strangers' ways replaced her past peace and solidarity. One might have thought the foreigners had permission to rape and plunder! Arrogantly, like packs of angry tigers, they trampled through once peaceful villages, murdering defenseless peasants, pillaging, stealing, claiming private lands and resources for themselves. The seizure of Manchuria was nearing the breaking point of China's patience. Her leader, Chiang Kai-shek, asserted his country had been pushed too far and launched strenuous efforts to improve the nation's military posture. It was openly public knowledge; Japan's armies tightened its death grip, and it had to stop.

The *Augusta* was conducting her usual training from Tsingtao when political and military events worsened. Main loudspeakers aboard the ship crackled and reported startling news. She was leaving China. The entire fleet was preparing for an immediate departure. For security reasons, the admiral shielded the exact time and date of separation. Still, the gravity of the situation was blatantly apparent: "Soldiers, sailors, airmen, marines, by now you should have made all necessary personal preparations for the evacuation of military dependents. If they have not already departed, they are to leave the country at once."

The dreaded confirmation shook Harold to the core. He was confident the news could not have come at a worse time. The new admiral's crisply stated words—cold, shocking, and sudden—reiterated Harold's worst fears. The solemnity and imminence of his personal situation struck him with terror. Everyone knew military orders were chiseled in stone. It was merely a matter of time before the *Augusta* weighed anchor. Time was no longer a friend. Harold knew it, as did all with loved ones not already out of the country. Though the fleet would be gone, even casual observers understood she wasn't going home. And, of course, the matter of transporting dependents aboard her was out of the question. By the end of the month, under sealed orders, the fleet would be gone.

Madelaine's dangerous situation ripped at Harold's gut as never before. "Sometime" was immediately translated as "no time." He couldn't, wouldn't, leave her, and he couldn't stay, nor could she. His patriotism—dedication to honor, duty, and country—and his responsibility to his family created a terrific dichotomy. Both duty and responsibility painfully tugged at him from opposing directions.

The world was shocked when sudden ultimatums ordered the immediate evacuation of all foreigners from Chinese soil. Scrambling and frantic refugees attempted to leave by every means possible, though ultimately, it was the invaders who made the final decisions regarding which individuals were allowed to leave, where they went, and those who were strictly forbidden to leave—period. Fleeing refugees needed official papers. Without documentation, life was a loaded crap game. Hastily constructed concentration camps were springing up all over the country. And it didn't take long to fill them, regardless of nationality.

Nations traditionally demanded the safe return of their citizens. However, the intolerant Germans demanded Jews from every country were to be transported only to the Deutschland. Chinese officials were eager to please, but Japan overruled orders and made final decisions about whom to ship where. Madelaine grieved when she heard Nina and Jacob and Jews from many nations were rounded up like sheep and herded into cattle cars, minus every personal thing of monetary value.

The doctors said they had done all they could for Madelaine and released her from the hospital with instructions to go home to the States immediately! Still plagued by morning sickness, injured, and very frightened, she and Harold huddled, trying to devise a plan. Having seen viciousness firsthand, they realized how deeply unprotected she and the baby were—and the gravity and dangers engulfing them—as if she didn't have enough for endless worry. Madelaine was drowning in stress and certainly in no condition to travel, but staying in China was not a reasonable option. In limbo—without funds, permission, or tickets to anywhere—she paced and wept.

"Harold, what are we gonna do? I can't see any way out. They'll kill me! We don't mean anything to them! I can't stop shakin'. We need answers, miracles ... and we need 'em now! There's no time for guessing or hoping." With tears wetting her pillow, she repeated the deepest fears and desires of her heart. "We have to have a miracle!"

Harold belonged to the navy. His only honorable choice was to follow orders, and yet he could not leave her. He already knew that any petition for help from his immediate superiors would most likely be met with grim, deliberate indifference—perhaps malicious mockery— because time was too short for assistance through the administrative processes. For the first time in their lives, the couple felt utterly frustrated, abandoned, and without hope.

It was after midnight when Madelaine whispered, "Harold, we'd better start praying with greater intensity. I can't think of any way out of this awful situation. Everything leaving China is already overbooked. There's no train or steamer with room for me at any price! Even if there was, we don't have the money! What are we going to do? I'm so scared. We need a miracle—and it won't wait. There's no time for guessing or hoping. If it's going to happen, we have to make it happen!"

As they slipped to their knees, Harold asked her to speak to God for both of them. He said he hardly dared ask for the kind of nearly impossible divine intervention so desperately needed. Prayer hadn't been a priority in Hal's life until now. But he did know God could manage anything. After all, He was keeping the sun and moon in their places, wasn't He? The Lord was indeed their only hope. Between weeping and desperation, Madelaine prayed for miracles, wisdom, protection, and survival for their growing family. They weren't essential to the world, she thought, but they were everything to each other. She blew her nose and wiped the tears. "Let's sleep on faith, sweetheart, knowing all things are possible with God. We've put our complete trust in His hands. I know He will open doors for us. Believe, sweetheart. Believe with all your heart and trust Him."

The night was long and starless, watered with tension, hopelessness, and trembling terror. They wept, reasoned, and paced until the wee hours of the morning. Harold found it impossible to sleep. He had too much on his mind. He held and rocked his anxious bride, reassuring her there was an answer. Hal said if God didn't know, nobody did. Still, this faith matter was something he'd never fully trusted—before now. He needed answers to unsolvable problems. Fear, confusion, and terrible dangers were eating him alive. How, he wondered, had life spun out of control so quickly?

When the morning sunlight streaked brightly across the room, Hal was still pondering, trying to unscramble his thoughts and options. He was only a seaman first-class fireman, but the answers, the certainty of what needed to transpire, came into Hal's heart as clearly as a fountain of clear stream water. It felt like a stroke of inspiration.

"Madelaine, I know what I have to do. First thing this morning, I'm jumpin' the chain of command." His decision was no small thing. It was an enormous toss of the dice. To go directly to the top brass risked becoming a pariah in the estimation of every single NCO and the full officers he intended to bypass.

His spirit whispered, "Risk it anyway." Harold immediately circumvented protocol and headed straight for the XO's office. There, with all a sailor's strength he could possibly muster, he explained the gravity of his situation and pleaded for help. His tearstained cheeks were an embarrassment. He truthfully added they had no money for contingencies. He then stood at attention, stared straight ahead, and took the reprimand respectfully, knowing the XO's chastisement was absolutely correct. Finally, Hal and the XO hastily composed an urgent memo:

USS *AUGUSTA*
Shanghai, China

October 10, 1940

From: FOLTZ, Harold W., Flc Ser, No 3334-11-48
TO: CinCAF
Via: Executive Office, USS *AUGUSTA*
Subject: Emergency Request - Transport of Spouse to the States

1. Request permission to have my wife transported to the States on the first available mode of transportation.
2. Reasons for the above are:

She suffered a severe and unfortunate fall and has been under a doctor's care since August 15, 1940. She is expecting a baby on or around the latter part of January. The doctors wish her to be in the States when the infant arrives.

I hope to be returning to the States aboard the USS *AUGUSTA* within several months. I would like to have my dependent family in the country on or before my arrival, if possible. I investigated commercial transportation and found passage on all ships booked up to and after the first of December, 1940.

I have sufficient funds available for her transportation.

Sincerely thanking you,
Harold W. Foltz, USN

Translation: It was a gamble, his last hope. Hal knew he didn't have sufficient funds. Truthfully, he had no funds at all, but he knew he had received an inspired idea, and this was it!

The XO promised he'd hand carry the urgent request on the double.

"I'll speak with Captain Magruder at once," he said, "but I can't promise you anything."

The skipper was very, very annoyed. But, hoping he could do something constructive, he gave his word to plead the cause. There weren't any guarantees the admiral or Japanese could or would grant an immediate safe passage out of China, even if she was already packed and ready to go. But orders were dispatched, marked *Urgent* and *Top Secret*. The captain immediately spoke with the admiral—Admiral Thomas C. Hart. He was at the top of the chain, next to God.

Hal felt the world lifting from his chest when the XO informed him an official reply had been received. Madelaine was cleared to leave. The admiral would find room for her and appraise the sailor and his dependent immediately when final arrangements were secured. Only then did Hal request emergency financial assistance. With future earnings, he promised to work off the debt for her transportation. Miraculously, his application was approved on the double. Her allotment check dropped to thirty-eight dollars a month. Hal wondered how anyone could live on such meager funds, but there wasn't time to quibble. They would find a way—and be eternally grateful for the blessings of miracles, home, freedom, prayer, life, and any check at all!

The brass hastily handstamped and signed papers to relieve Harold's desperate situation. A messenger from the admiral's flagship promptly delivered copies of them to Japanese officials. They stated a pregnant US Navy dependent was granted permission to sail for the United States the following day and report to the Japanese Customs Office at 0830. She was granted permission to board an overloaded American vessel waiting for her, bound for the United States of America.

Harold and Madelaine knelt again and placed their lives, their futures, their all in the hands of the Almighty. Hal kissed his frightened wife and tearfully embraced the devoted, faithful houseboy. With faith and a heavy, trusting heart, he left Madelaine in Yong's care and reported for duty in the boiler room aboard the USS *Augusta*. Yong wept as they hurriedly packed the last box of treasures, including a blue silk baby book for their 'Melican baby, his personal gift. Trembling, he promised he would take her to the dock and pledged every way possible to protect her.

The following morning when they arrived, the Japanese officials threatened to shoot him as Madelaine looked into Yong's tearful eyes and whispered, "Get out of here! Leave now! Run!" She'd already handed off all the yuan they had. He would surely need it. Her tears and heavy heart said what everyone already absolutely knew. It was a nominal price for the devoted, loving service Yong so honorably and generously rendered.

The rest was in God's hands.

CHAPTER 11

Clarity at Sea

Who's That Man? 1941

Madelaine stood on the bow of the ship, uncertain, frightened, and alone. Gazing at the rolling sea, she covered her facial droopiness with her hand and a silk scarf. Hardly noticing other passengers, she was wholly absorbed in her thoughts. She wondered when she'd last eaten, sure if she'd eaten at all, she'd have lost it by now.

She brooded, agonizing at the probable fates of friends, Nina, Jacob, and Yong. Had they escaped the threatened terrors of war and found passage somehow to somewhere safely, elusive as that might be—some time, someplace? Where was Harold's ship? Was he safe? Madelaine grew sick with worry, piling questions upon one another. Answers were as vaporous as the seafoam blowing in the wind. Beside herself with grief, tears suddenly rained down her cheeks. Genuinely discouraged and depressed, she dabbed at the errant flow.

Absorbed in her private world, she only mildly noted a tall, thin man with soft gray hair watching from afar. Suddenly, he was standing beside her in silence. The gentleman asked if he could be of service. Madelaine was physically and emotionally exhausted. She blurted the entire story and added, "And I don't even know where he is!" Of course, she didn't. Orders were orders sealed and stamped *Top Secret*. Only

Harold understood what it meant to be aboard a warship, under orders, heading full steam into a foggy bank of ambiguity.

The stranger was quiet, deep in thought, and listening intently to her tearful narrative. He was discreet, asking unusual questions, such as what kind of vessel Harold boarded, exactly where it had been moored, and if she knew the name or hull numbers. She did. Holding his raised binoculars, he shifted uneasily. Turning starboard momentarily, the stranger removed the binoculars from his eyes and pointed his finger into the wind.

"Do you see that ship ahead of us?"

She looked in the direction he indicated. In the distance, dark, unmistakable smoke from a steaming vessel rambled aimlessly on the wind.

Blinking, she responded, "Yes."

The gentleman's eyes suspiciously surveyed the deck around them, noting every passenger's position and demeanor within sight. He then handed the binoculars to Madelaine. She looked at him with curiosity, adjusted the glasses, and peered ahead. Hoping for less conspicuousness, he whispered, "Keep your eyes on that ship. It's an important vessel on a vitally urgent mission—with a special crew." As she stared through the borrowed binoculars, the distant gray craft steamed on. Clearly, she was a military warship in a hurry.

"Look at the numbers on the hull," the stranger prodded. "Can you read them?"

Madelaine strained all the harder. Suddenly, the distant vessel made a course correction, and the numbers were no longer visible. She watched as it moved farther and farther in the distance. And when only a speck remained, the two passengers gazed in turn through binoculars at the restless whitecaps and bottomless sea. The dot disappeared. Turning her attention to the stranger, she hoped to read his mind, but an invisible lock read Closed. Who was that man? she wondered. What did he know of hull numbers and the locations and names of ships at sea?

He didn't say. Madelaine was unaware he'd boarded before she did. Perhaps he noted her late arrival, the unusual circumstances, or edgy soldiers escorting her to the gangplank. Impressed and comforted,

Madelaine sniffled discreetly in the crisp, salty air as a sudden feeling of peace and calmness overcame her.

She'd seen Harold's vessel!

She couldn't explain how she knew, but she knew, and her heart leaped, knowing they were sharing the same glassy sea on a small planet in a grand and glorious galaxy. The stranger smiled and nodded knowingly. He then retrieved his expensive binoculars and walked away.

Madelaine's cabin was small, crowded, and stale smelling. Neither the rolling sea nor cramped quarters eased the queasiness in her stomach. But she did her best in the stillness of the night to count her blessings, ponder, and ignore the harrowing experiences of an uncertain, unfriendly evacuation. Though it was late, she grabbed a jacket and again headed topside. She was hoping for one more look at the brilliant stars and midnight sea, fairly certain a breath of fresh air would assuage her restlessness.

Her face was numb, and the cool breezes felt good. The mesmerizing sight of millions of celestial bodies sparkling in the night sky warmed her heart. Following imagined dares, she lifted her hand to pluck a falling star and held it to her breast. She was confident the lights in the heavens were speaking to her, begging to be wished upon. Quietly, she obliged.

When absolutely sure she was utterly alone, convinced only God was aware of her, she bespoke her silent thoughts, convinced the wind would carry them onward.

She thought of Harold's youthful saga, capturing fireflies in glass jars on hot Ohio evenings, and of his love for and devotion to her. The quiet surroundings comforted her, bringing angelic solitude, reminding her how close she felt to Deity—how similar her shared feelings were for God and her beloved husband.

Though life in Oregon, at home and with family, felt light-years away, her mind danced at thoughts of berry picking and merriment. She could almost taste the soft, tart fruit from vines along the family's fence. Leaning on the rail of the ship, she marveled at the unrivaled beauty of the night. Except for the sounds of the sea and the wind in her ears, the world was silent and comforting.

Might her sweetheart be standing on the bridge of the *Augusta* somewhere, thinking of her and wishing on the same happy stars?

Unexpectedly, the baby moved. Feelings of unborn life were reassuring. She knew the two of them were safe in the palm of God's hand. She sighed deeply, wholly assured He knew where they were and was designing futures yet to be revealed.

It would be months before Harold received Madelaine's onionskin letter. And when he did, he was shocked to learn the extreme danger she'd faced and her bravery. He knew for a fact that many civilians were being imprisoned or killed because they had no means of escape.

The dangerous and unkindly interactions Madelaine faced with the arrogant, nasty foreign officials took his breath away. He believed her words when she wrote angels were traveling with her, but he was terribly upset not to have been able to render significant assistance—to have been more forceful on her behalf, more protective. He pondered his inspired audacity for hastily scribbling a memo to the admiral. It truly had made a difference. He knew he had followed divinely inspired prompting to have been so forward. Just maybe, he reflected, her name on some exclusive petition with USN beside it had saved her life. It had been a close call.

Harold could not have known Yong would place himself in extreme danger protecting and aiding his injured charge. He wished the faithful houseboy knew the full extent of gratitude for a friend who undoubtedly saved Madelaine's life and that of the unborn child. What words adequately expressed Hal's thoughts? Madelaine's last and chaotic days in China were unfathomably frightening and cruel. From their first meeting, Harold knew Yong was an extraordinary man. Logic and faith helped assure Hal's belief there was a God up there, somewhere, guarding and protecting those whom Hal loved. Humbled, he prayed for faithful people everywhere, especially those who dared to place others' welfare above their own.

History recorded a long and ugly war that blanketed Yong and millions of others with depravity and unimaginable horror. In her heart of hearts, Madelaine was aware her life had been spared by divine intervention, and in quiet moments, she often pondered the fate of others trapped in her situation. Miraculously, the overloaded passenger ship with no room for even one more passenger found a place for just one more. She was going home.

Yong had nowhere to go. Under a canopy of stars, Madelaine prayed for him and recalled her own heavenly gifts. She never forgot the harsh Japanese pronouncement meant to be final: there's no room for another evacuee.

And the stranger? Curiously, Madelaine never knew his true identity. Elusive as he was, he didn't say. Still, undoubtedly he was someone who had an unusual amount of privilege, foreknowledge, and intelligence about the military, world affairs, international law, politics, intrigue, wars, the Japanese army, and troops' and ships' movements at sea.

It just might have been more than fate that a stranger took particular interest in an unborn child and a young, frightened navy dependent destined for motherhood in America. Madelaine pondered the man's final words and calmly whispered her gratitude to the stars in the gentle wind. She never forgot how extremely fortunate she was to have known "a seemingly insignificant Chinaman" as Yong and Godly intervention.

Miraculously, she stood alone, sailing on one of the last ships to leave China—bound for freedom and motherhood in the United States of America.

CHAPTER 12

One Dock at a Time

San Francisco, California, 1940

The SS *Washington*,[2] tired from a long voyage at sea, sailed proudly under the Golden Gate and maneuvered dockside. Dona, the youngest of Madelaine's siblings, jumped with glee, her bobby socks in perpetual motion. Squealing, she pointed to a small figure at the railing of the ship: "Look, look! There she is. I see her! That's Madelaine. She's home!"

Ambling down the gangplank, many weary travelers dropped their heavy luggage and rested momentarily on the dock. Madelaine pushed the limp hair from her face, straightened her royal blue knitted suit, and smiled. It was good to be in freedom's lap again. If she hadn't been so exhausted, she'd have kissed the ground. Instead, she shared an abundance of hugs and tears with family, overjoyed at the sight of familiar faces and home. But she was thin and haggard, her face tattle-telling of a ghastly accident abroad. Her appearance was shocking. She'd written about the pregnancy but not the fall.

"Throwing up for thirty-five hundred rolling miles takes its toll," she crowed. "A little rest, and I'll be fine. I'd like to see a navy doctor as soon as possible. I need to know if what I'm feeling is normal, that the baby is all right—and, um—see what they can do for my face." She added the doctors in China said the appalling paralysis could be

---

[2] A luxury ocean liner, passenger capacity 1083, emergency contingency 1787.

temporary—they hoped. Of course, Dona wanted to know everything at once—the fall, foreign intrigue, the Asian people and customs, the unborn baby, sightseeing in the ancient lands, and every aspect of married life abroad. Someday she hoped to travel, just like her big sister. Madelaine explained leaving China was far more complicated than getting there in the first place.

She asked the girls to help locate the rest of her belongings and reassured them there'd be plenty of time to talk later. She winked and added Dona might want to think twice about living overseas, no matter how exhilarating the idea sounded. She said, "Dorothy was right when she told Toto there's no place like home!" And, Madelaine added, there were plenty of surprises in her steamer trunk!

The skyline was familiar, as if she'd never left—except for missing Harold. Arduous ship-life stories and the quiet man with the binoculars could wait, though Madelaine hoped to introduce him to her family. Satisfied she'd seen him disembark, she warily surveyed the crowd and deduced he'd vanished as mysteriously as he first appeared. "Oh, never mind," she told herself. "We'll get to that later."

Elaine stood silently with a toddler in her arms. The two-year-old with beautiful pale skin was quiet, curious, and sweet. She watched her aunts and others, all chattering in unison. Dark ringlets and soft ribbons framed the child's face. The tot resembled her great-grandmother's French-Canadian ancestry. The child's large brown eyes pierced the souls of onlookers, and her smile was infectious. Baby Janice, a placid little thing, was easy to love. Dona considered the child her personal play doll. Shyly, little Janice smiled at Madelaine. As part of a large and loving family, Madelaine wasn't a gushy mother-to-be, but she returned the smile and touched the baby's tiny hand. Thoughts came of her own pregnancy, of the possibility she might be carrying a little girl. In her heart, Madelaine wished for a handsome, blue-eyed boy much like little Buddy, but a daughter would do. She just wanted them healthy and normal.

Amid the chatter, she looked at the pavement, American soil—and a shipload of very fortunate travelers. Pausing, she took a deep breath and relished the unmistakable scent of the moist, salty air. Intuition whispered everything necessary and vital that had to do with love, and family was hers.

Then, pausing in deep reflection, she remembered having stood with Harold in the very place where she now stood alone. Loneliness rekindled the painful separation in her heart, but faith buoyed her hope that time would take care of everything. The tedious exodus from China had left her courage meter reading half-empty. She thought of the ship packed with extremely lucky evacuees. It was more than the pregnancy and paralysis that was bothering her. With only the beauty of the stars for comfort, the stress and monotony and the vessel's never-ending ship noise and motion had made deep and meaningful rest periods difficult.

The sisters said their Nordic ancestry should have been helpful. Madelaine giggled, thought of an incident at sea, and said that every good Norsewoman should know to first check the direction of the wind before heaving overboard!

Donna grimaced. "Oh no, you didn't ... did you?"

Though the worldwide news wasn't improving, firsthand reports from home seemed worse. No one had written that their beloved parents were separated, contemplating a divorce! Madelaine had never heard a cross word between them. Their home life seemed rich and harmonious, centered in faith and strong family loyalties. Together they'd borne all things as a unit—the Great Depression, disappointments, the sting of burying loved ones, economics and health issues. The family had always crossed those bridges together—their motto being "Family first!"

And now? It seemed they'd reached the River of Defeat without safety nets, giving up on each other, on the family. Divorce? "We didn't know how to tell you," the group confessed.

Madelaine's jaw dropped as she looked from sister to sister, to her mother and the baby. She could not find words to express her shock, her disbelief. She pressed her hands to her head and tried to push the thought, the loss of her beloved family unit, to the furthest recesses of her mind. Indeed, time would mend broken dreams. Perhaps they'd listen to her and reason things out ...

Throughout the following days, she cried, preached, and reasoned, but nothing dissuaded the resolve of her parents' decision. She concluded it was excruciating to watch a family implode, especially one's own.

Shattered dreams, hopes, lives ... Madelaine's heart ached as she disclosed the news in a letter to Harold.

"You and I must always work things out. We vowed there'd be no room in our lives for divorce. I don't ever want to hear the word spoken in our home. Never!" she wrote.

"Deal," he replied. "Never, never, never."

CHAPTER 13

Shabby Chic

Oakland, California, 1941

It wasn't easy to support one's sick, lonely, expectant self on thirty-eight dollars a month. Tokens for the trolly, stationery, and a few extra coins for maternity needs very quickly gobbled up the balance of funds. Madelaine was learning to juggle reality and frugality like an acrobat, but above all, she was grateful to be home again.

Harold told the admiral he did have funds to pay her way to the States—until the official wanted to see the dollar amount he'd saved written on paper. The awful truth was he'd be pressed to come up with twenty dollars, let alone the needed fare. Though not in the habit of habitually *fudging*, Hal hadn't been entirely truthful with his superiors until it was almost too late. He was frightened and worried about his injured pregnant wife, and he reasoned piling on an additional request for money, on top of everything else, would cause the entire matter to be stoutly refused. She had to leave the Orient immediately, even at the cost of fudging. The baby wasn't going to wait.

Pulling emergency strings, the admiral persuaded the navy to loan Hal the difference between what he had (in his empty pocket) and what she needed. The funds were to be repaid, of course, every cent—with interest. And so the navy bought a one-way-ticket for her and deducted the cost from the already meager dependent's allotment she received monthly. Hal knew the debt was going to drag on until every penny was repaid. In the meantime, she would just have to make do with what was left. Getting settled in could have been much more complicated than it was, but as luck would have it, Madelaine was riding high.

Shortly after docking in the bay, she was fortunate to meet with the doctors at the Oak Knoll Naval Hospital. Her dragon luck was still holding as she explained her recent harrowing ordeals, the injury, and trying to leave China before being rounded up and interred in a Japanese concentration camp. Most likely, she wouldn't have lived.

As luck held, a kindly nurse charged with taking the patient's vitals was listening sympathetically as her patient described the desperation they faced. It was a totally unexpected surprise when the nurse invited the frightened patient to become her live-in guest—for the time being. Extremely grateful, Madelaine thanked her and tearfully accepted the generous offer. The two women instantly bonded. Both were military wives with deployed husbands.

"Just call me Debby," said the nurse. "I think you'll like my place. It's not fancy, but the rent is reasonable. While I'm working, you'll have plenty of privacy and a comfortable place to rest. I could use a little company once in a while. I get tired of talking to myself—and the pictures on the wall."

"Me too," Madelaine replied. "It should just be temporary. I'll be looking for a place of our own before the baby comes, and Harold may have some shore duty. But who knows when that might be! I want to have a little place of our own as soon as possible."

On days off, the friends cleaned the apartment, giggled, and chatted. They shared public military news and did their best to stay informed about the ship and air movements broadcasting on public airwaves.

In her off shifts, Debby removed her nurse's cap but never abandoned sensitivities to Madelaine's plight. She freely shared advice and optimism—"Things will work out." Meeting a good friend at the hospital was just another tender mercy that arrived when Madelaine needed it most. Sharing rent, utilities, and groceries was helpful—one less thing about which to worry. Debby said she'd heard of paralytic reversals and encouraged "Maddy" to be patient. She was sure there were urgent matters of greater importance than attaching useless worry to their psyches.

"You'll probably be delivering your baby at Mare Island," Debby said. "Plenty of water and rest will do wonders. That's what you need, and less stress over things for which we have no jurisdiction—none at all!"

Madelaine knew the temporary living arrangement was a ticking clock. She poured through newspapers, searching for an affordable nest of her own, and was elated when persistence paid off. One morning as she was perusing the *Chronicle*, there it was, "For Rent: cheap, cut-rate unit (in a dangerous and shabby part of town), no amenities."

Debby was ecstatic when it was announced her flier husband was due home for a short visit. Repacking Madelaine's few items was easy, and the move went smoothly. The gals promised the distance would never disrupt their friendship. And indeed, the two remained close friends throughout their lives.

The meeting with the prospective landlord went well. Madelaine signed the agreement on the spot. She borrowed a hotplate and a pan, and they served her well. Without refrigeration, bread, fresh fruit, and raw vegetables were stored well on a small counter. Sugar, meat, and most canned goods were rationed anyway. For furniture, Madelaine scrounged the neighborhood and discovered an old fruit crate. She painted it white and mounted it on the kitchen wall.

"That will do," she told herself. "It will be just fine for a few plates and a couple of bowls from the Five and Dime ..." and whatever else she could afford. When the carpentry work was finished, she stepped back and admired her resourcefulness.

Refrigeration was quite a weightier matter. It would become even more pressing when the baby arrived. Though she didn't have an icebox, Madelaine memorized the route of the neighborhood ice man. Following the truck, she gathered unwanted shards as the truck rambled from house to house. She placed the ice chips in the sink and covered them with a towel. "Clever," she uttered.

The new area was not safe, but out of necessity, she walked a couple of blocks to the neighborhood store in broad daylight, carefully juggling her purchases with coins and rationing coupons. Each week, she squirreled away a few precious ingredients. She was saving them for a surprise for Harold. He said the crew aboard the ship always complained about the tasteless meals from the galley. Hal hoarded the few coffee cans of goodies like other lucky sailors—mostly stale cookies or hardened fudge when something from home arrived.

The cooks took the complaints on the cuff. After all, they explained, they weren't to blame for the delays in replenishing supplies! Oh, it wasn't just the food over which the sailors grumbled. It was wartime, and nothing was predictable: the delivery of the mail, news from home, or canned meat.

Madelaine had ideas she hoped would bring a little joy to Harold's finicky stomach. She was storing goodies when she could find them, one extra can at a time.

And they said it was impossible to live on thirty-eight dollars a month!

CHAPTER 14

Cookin' at Sea

And a Bundle in a Basket, 1941

Though often disturbed by their contents, Madelaine was anxious to open the infrequent letters from Harold. They never revealed the movements of ships or where they'd been. But Hal spoke of the frightening encounters at sea, blasts of the sixteen-inch guns, and horrifying sounds of enemy torpedoes in the water—near misses. Of course, he had heartfelt complaints about missing her, home, and family.

He was curious about Madelaine's new friend, Debby, grateful she'd been so helpful. He wanted to know what kind of a place Madelaine had rented and how she was stretching her monthly allotment. And he agonized over his chief complaint, the food at sea.

Quick and inventive, Madelaine avoided ticklish subjects. She asked if he could do any cooking in the boiler room. Not wanting to worry him about things over which they had no control, she told herself she'd get to the matter of the money and her new living quarters later.

And yes, her pregnancy was blossoming naturally.

He chuckled at the sooty idea of cooking in the boiler room and replied, "There ain't nothin' in this place but piles of coal and enough dust and heat to make a gorilla go bald!" Hal was proud of his shiny, dark hair and—um—planned to tell her about the thinning issue sometime in the future. He hoped it wouldn't make a difference.

"There ain't much ventilation in the boiler room," he wrote back, "and no good way to get the oppressive heat outta here when we're steamin'. Sweatin' keeps us wet and thin, though we're constantly pourin' water down our gullets. Well, hon, about the grub … Since you asked, it's terrible!"

"Harold," Madelaine said, "I've got an idea that might bring a little whiff of home to you as you're sailing. As you know, my mom had a big family, five living kids, freeloading relatives, boarders, bums, and very little money. She regularly made purses out of sows' ears and worked miracles in the kitchen. She always fed drifters and anyone else who was hungry and in need of a good meal. I'm savin' canned goods for you and swapping rationing coupons for more. If you can open the cans, mix the stuff together, and heat it up in the boiler, I'm betting you'll love a nice pot of homemade soup. At least it will remind you how much you're thought of and should help keep your love for me pipin' hot!"

Hal scratched his head and thought deeply. He'd need a pot for the soup, but his duty station was the boiler room, not the galley, and the cook wasn't willing to share anything but complaints and a bad temper most of the time. Supplies were really scarce. Hal thought if he had a way of cleaning one of the coal shovels, it just might work.

"Honey, I got an idea. Do you have any pot scrubbers? If you can find some, will ya send 'em with the cans?" And so she did.

Assembling a fine collection of ingredients and her original recipe, she enclosed a couple of rough scouring pads and some scrubbing powder. It would take time for the box to reach Harold's ship, wherever it was, but her faith said the soup was going to be a winner.

Madelaine routinely looked for and greeted the postman warmly. But she was not fond of the questions he continually asked: "Where's the ship now?" Everybody knew loose lips sank ships—everyone except the nosy postman.

One day, the letter she was waiting for finally arrived. Hal was full of joy. He'd managed to polish the bed of a coal shovel, opened the cans, poured everything into his makeshift kettle, and shoved the whole thing into the raging boiler. Carefully, he followed her directions.

Corn Willie

2 cans of green beans with juice
2 cans of corn with juice
2 cans of peas, drained
3 cans of sliced potatoes, drained
1 can of corned beef
Some dried onions
2 cans of chopped tomatoes with juice
Add a can of tomato sauce,
Several cans of water
Salt and pepper

It didn't take long for the aroma to filter throughout the ship. Curious sailors wondered if they were hallucinating. Soon a line of men followed their noses through the narrow passageways, past the galley, picking up steam on the way to the boiler room.

"Foltz, where's them smells comin' from?"

The unwanted company made Harold nervous. "What smells?" he replied.

It suddenly occurred to him a spoon and bowl would be useful, so he fessed up and said, "If you ole birds can come up with somethin' to eat it with, I'll show ya what I got."

The stampede to the galley caused a traffic jam of monumental proportions as eager diners made U-turns and trampled past hitherto uninformed sailors in the tight passageway.

"Watchu call it?" the men asked. "And where'd you get this stuff?" Harold was popular! Even the XO and several chiefs traipsed to the boiler room to share the tasty meal.

"Son," said the chief, "this is absolutely delicious. It's full of vegetables, and the aroma is magnificent. The cook wants to know if he can have the recipe."

"Sir, he can have a bowl full, but I ain't sharin' the recipe. It's my wife's secret, and I gotta keep it that way, or she won't be sending me no more cans. No more fudge or cookies either!"

Madelaine laughed out loud when she received his letter, imagining Harold polishing the heavy black coal shovel until it was clean and shiny. She knew the soup's aroma very well and made it as frequently as she could horde the right ingredients.

"Honey," he wrote, "whatcha call that soup? All the guys wanna know."

"I named it Corn Willie."

"Corn Willie? Where'd you come up with that name?"

"Silly. Willie, after you, (Harold *William*) and Willie Lump-Lump, the popular cartoon character. And, well, everyone knows the soup is full of corn! I packed some extra corn just for you."

Harold blushed when he announced to the crew, without a lot of explanation, his master creation was called, uh, Corn Willie! He didn't explain the Willie Lump-Lump story, a wildly popular cartoon character in the Sunday funnies. Willie was always bumbling around. He was not a competent handyman, unable to fix anything the right way, though he was still trying—someone who never did anything the easy way.

Madelaine teased Hal with Willie's nickname, and it stuck—a private joke between the two of them.

"Harold William," Madelaine wrote, "don't take it too seriously, but sometimes you remind me of, uh, Willie Lump-Lump when you sort of go through a lot of extra gyrations that are really not necessary, trying to help out, and it doesn't work. I love you anyway. And now that you are a master chef at sea, winner of the most popular dish in the fleet, I love you even more!"

Though letters were infrequent, usually full of pining for home and loved ones, military families and the world at large most frequently obtained news through the faceless voices emanating from wooden radios. Madelaine seldom missed the broadcasts. Wanting to know about his vessel, she stuck pins into a map taped to the kitchen wall and checked the postmarks on Harold's latest letters. She devoured the *Chronicle*, looking for even a hint of where the ship carrying her sweetheart might be.

She waited for his notes and wrote long letters every night. "My dearest, darling Husband." With her trusty fountain pen, alone in the silence of the room, she penned her most profound thoughts on sweet-smelling stationery. Sometimes she enclosed rose petals from the neighbor's garden, pressed violets, or wild daisies. She whispered,

"He loves me; he loves me not. He loves me ..." She remembered his words; living without her was hardly worth the trouble. She frequently replenished bottles of ink—brown, black, red, green, and navy blue.

Some evenings, dressed in a skimpy black negligee, she combed her hair and applied bright red lipstick. She said it was important to look her best because she planned to dream about him. When she finished her letter writing, she yawned sleepily, licked her smooth red lips, and kissed the envelope, whispering quietly, "I love you, dear," wanting him to remember things as they'd been. If she could only know for sure he was safe—just some word about where he was, how he was, and when he'd be home again.

Scuttlebutt said that the *Augusta* was coming into Mare Island for an overhaul sometime in January 1941. It was only a rumor, but gossip was better than nothing, she thought. That's where she'd wait for him, almost comfortably in the Bay Area. It would have been nice to have lived closer to her mother and sisters, but they preferred the warmer Sacramento Valley, miles northeast of San Francisco. She couldn't stand the thought of being so far from the bases, from Harold's possible expected or unexpected visits.

Thus, her social calls to Sacramento were infrequent. But in her letters, Madelaine wrote lightly of her adjustments, international news, and suppositions. She licked the onionskin envelopes and mailed them as frequently as possible. She honestly lacked the money for penny stamps more than a few times a month but made up for it by stuffing several letters into one envelope, gleeful a single stamp would do.

When the ship finally tied up at Mare Island in January as predicted, Madelaine's delight was heavier than usual. Together at last on American soil, the couple shared a very pregnant reunion and plans for a rosy future when the war was finally over.

"Now, let me see." Harold grinned. "Where were we before we were so rudely interrupted?" However, the evening plans were rerouted as the couple raced to the maternity ward at the naval hospital on Mare Island.

Madelaine's water broke on Valentine's Day, 1941. Through the long, dark night, Harold paced and worried. Laboring through contractions and sweat, Madelaine confided to all within earshot that her mother never suffered any labor pains, none at all. Midwives were dubious until the babies slipped quietly into the world. Unfortunately, it was a phenomenon not passed onto her daughters. Struggling, Madelaine groaned on.

When the sun rose the following day, a new twig on the family tree was miraculously ordinary. They named her Nancy Lee Foltz—Yang Yuan Li in Chinese. She tipped the scales at just over six pounds, and Madelaine recorded it carefully in her blue silk baby book. At last, the months of worry about possible health issues for the baby were over. Still, the doctors were hopeful time would improve the mother's facial paralysis. Perhaps another pregnancy.

In the spotless nursery, the overprotective navy nurses scrutinized Hal's every movement. A brand-new father, he peeked shyly at his magnificent creation in a bassinet. Her red, swollen face and squinty eyes gave her a profoundly Oriental look.

Unintentionally imitating his mother, Harold blushed and said, "Jus' an itty-bitty thang, ain't she?" The infant was the first baby he'd ever held. Slowly, the grinning sailor kissed his little girl and examined the tiny fingers and toes. He told the watchful nurse he was looking for something, most probably stamped on her buttocks.

"You won't find *anything* stamped on that infant!" came the stern and impatient reply.

"Oh yes I will," Hal whispered to himself. "Made in China." He knew it for a fact!

CHAPTER 15

No Crib for a Bed

West Oakland, California, 1940–1941

She almost stretched the allotment check to the end of the month. In any sailor's book, Madelaine was a financial wizard. But when baby made three, the addition put a massive strain on an already difficult situation. Living stateside on love and a meager stipend was more than a significant inconvenience. Even shopping became an artform. She said if they could get along without it, they did. If they couldn't, they did it anyway.

With the war in full swing, few people had funds to make ends meet—especially military families in the minuscule complex Madelaine called home. The strains of life and shared poverty made keeping up with the Jones easy. Nobody wanted much more than an end to war and loved ones protected and returned safely home.

Though Harold was a responsible young father, home on leave, trying to pay the bills and support his family, the simple truth was he couldn't. The facts brought on major anxieties, and his frequently upset stomach refused to disappear. His inability to pay for desperately needed necessary supplies was like a vice around his acidic esophagus.

"Don't worry about the baby," Madelaine said.

She was thankful she could nurse—that is, until a yeast infection set in and the milk ran dry. But with a newborn in a dresser drawer and shortages staring them in the face, it wasn't long before the need for fresh milk reached a critical stage. The infant cried as worried parents brainstormed and borrowed nickels and dimes from generous friends.

Madelaine said it was a stroke of genius that whispered to her, "Put a note on an empty baby bottle and set it afloat." She was up to her elbows in a pan of sudsy dishwater when the thought came again. Suddenly she recognized the impression for what it was and knew what needed to be done. Of course, she could hardly wait to share the inspiration with Harold. As he stressfully rubbed his receding hairline, the couple counseled together in the tiny kitchen. He pondered the thought, unsure how to proceed.

"Do you really think it'll work?" the sailor asked dubiously.

"I know it will. I just know it's what we need to do."

The following day, Harold's heart was again swollen with angst. He held out the empty baby bottle with a note carefully attached to it and took another leap of faith. It wasn't easy expressing his desperation to the XO, but the understanding man gave permission to place the bottle aboard the ship "and see what happens!"

Madelaine's hand-printed note said it all: "Milk for the baby."

Brothers-in-arms dropped extra pocket change into the empty container. And at the end of the day, the bottle was filled and heavy. Harold attached the nipple, grinned, and joyfully carried the treasure home. When the milk and the money disappeared, he returned the bottle to the ship, and the generous sailors refilled it with nickels and dimes. Occasionally, a dollar bill appeared; it had *officer* tacitly written all over it.

The crew empathized with the baby's needs and considered it a joint venture to care for the elusive tot. They often stopped the young papa in the passageways, inquiring about the baby's weight and health. Even the single men called the little one theirs and asked to see the latest black-and-white photos. Collectively, they chuckled at the chubby results of their liberal contributions. Surprised, they snickered when Harold told them how comfortable she was in a small dresser drawer, aptly serving as a cradle. Cuddly pillows and a downy blanket kept her comfortable.

"Foltz, that ain't no respectable place for a baby!" the chief said.

"Well, it's workin' just fine, for now, sir," Hal replied.

Fortunately, when the baby outgrew the dresser drawer, the bathtub served as a doesn't-matter-wet-proof toddler bed. The steep porcelain sides made it impossible for the tot to climb in or out. Madelaine placed soft blankets in the tub and dangled toys from the water pipes to entertain her. When the need for bathing arose, her made-it-myself bed was out of commission and temporarily relocated.

During nap times, Madelaine faithfully wrote in the Shanghai-purchased baby book, covered with navy blue silk. She pasted her own baby pictures next to the smiling, moon-faced, pigtailed Chinese cutouts. The little book always reminded her of their hasty departure, "the bum's rush" she called it, and of its gracious giver: Yong.

Hurriedly, he'd wrapped the gift in tissue paper and tucked it in the bottom of her suitcase. He choked on his words and wagged his finger: "Missy hab good 'Melican baby, easy hurt." With his head bobbing, he reassured her, "Gud face com back OK. I see yu sum-time, otter day." They both knew the war would change everything forever. She sighed and remembered how thorny the evacuation had been, how dangerously close she was to becoming just another statistic marked unknown. Yong literally risked his life for her, for the baby. She closed the book and gently stroked the delicate silk.

Madelaine was fortunate to have so many young couple neighbors like themselves—mostly military people, coming and going, swapping scuttlebutt, personal experiences, roomers, rationing coupons, and the like. It wasn't a secret; the flat wasn't in the best part of town, but it was almost affordable and their own.

On most days, the fog rolled quietly over the bay. By late afternoon, things were quiet and wet again. Just as she settled herself comfortably with a good book on the used sofa, with intentions of resting while the baby slept, she was suddenly caught off guard by a sharp rap on the door. Straightening her hair with one hand, she reached for the doorknob with the other.

A kindly down-the-hall neighbor invited herself into the barren unit. She'd heard about the baby bottle on the ship and the need for purchased milk. She looked Madelaine in the eye, introduced herself, then bowed her head and mumbled she was aware they were struggling with a way to keep the baby's milk from spoiling. She knew the shards of ice Madelaine collected from the idling ice truck hardly did the job.

"We have a little extra space in our icebox," the neighbor said. "Why don't you consider storing it at our place?" She beamed.

Though the neighbor's wooden icebox was tiny, there was ample room for the baby's needs. Madelaine was excited and thanked her thoughtful new friend. She said she'd check with Harold and get back to her right away!

"We need our own icebox," Harold said, moaning, "and a stove and a washing machine!" Though he was appreciative of the offer, frustration was taking its toll. Wet diapers hung throughout the apartment, and it hurt him to see what the harsh soap was doing to Madelaine's pretty hands.

"It's the lye," she said. The soap recipe was her mother's, made from leftover cooking grease. Harold rolled his eyes and brooded. He could do without, but he wanted better things for his family. They deserved it. He was increasingly moody and disappointed in his inability to afford even a blasted bar of store-bought soap!

Why was it when they reached their greatest disappointments, Madelaine always thought of prayer? He wasn't raised that way, Harold said.

"Honey," she replied, "when there's nobody else to turn to, there's always God. He hasn't let us down yet."

It was getting harder to separate wants from needs. To further complicate matters, Madelaine said she wanted to donate to the church! She reminded Harold they could use some divine assistance, and they already owed an enormous debt of gratitude to Deity.

"What *extra* money?" Harold groused in response. "You want to give the milk money away? Does anyone need it more than we do? My wallet has more holes in it than Swiss cheese! We don't have a dime to our name. How can we afford to give anything away? We got less than nothin' to give anybody—nothin'!"

Madelaine never gave up 'til she wore him down. She said the donation had more to do with faith than funds. "I think we need to take these important matters to someone higher than the navy." Then, looking at the baby, she smiled and said softly, "Faith is a belief in things not seen but hoped for, and a chubby, well-nourished baby is proof. Look at those tubby legs."

Harold complained. Not a churchgoer, he often leaned on her insights for spiritual counsel. She reminded him how generous the sailors were, donating money for the miracle milk so desperately needed, of her miraculous escape from the war-torn Orient, and bombardments at sea narrowly missing their mark. He'd heard the earth-shattering whistle of enemy torpedoes speeding through the sea, headed for his ship. It was horrifying, especially from the boiler room at the bottom of the vessel. He knew at any moment death could become a certainty. How was it possible for the enemy to have missed? Madelaine said God had protected him, and He was listening to their passionate, heartfelt prayers.

"The bottle money's a great blessing," she continued, "and a tithe is just a small way of expressing thanks, faith, and gratitude. I know it works. I've done it all my life." Harold wasn't totally convinced sharing what little they had was prudent, but he agreed to think about it before he said no.

"Pray about it?" she coaxed.

Harold didn't know any prayers except the hasty, hair-raising expressions uttered in the boiler room in the belly of the ship. The combat was terrifying. He knew plenty of those prayers but seriously doubted there was any correlation between paying a tithe, as Madelaine suggested, and safeguarding the meager funds so desperately needed.

Madelaine whispered, "It's worth a try, isn't it? What do we have to lose? Let's trust this matter to the Lord."

That evening, the couple knelt awkwardly by the side of the bed. Madelaine asked Harold to trust the Lord and speak to him as though He was in the same room, man-to-man, talking and listening. Crouching in the light of a small, bedside lamp, the two of them knelt, and Harold poured out his soul. It was good to speak aloud the things that were gnawing at him. He said what God already knew; his family was suffering, and there was no money for nothin'.

Dispirited, he said he was working extra hard, long hours to support them—but he couldn't make ends meet. As an afterthought, he pushed his luck and blurted out how greatly they needed a miracle to keep the milk fresh. He said emergency runs to the neighbor's icebox in the middle of the night were embarrassing. "And," he continued, "if you've got an extra icebox up there, we could sure use it!"

One might argue it was merely a coincidence, but the following morning, an elated across-the-hall neighbor rushed to Madelaine's door and rapped loudly. Excitedly, she announced her husband had been transferred, and she was following the ship to San Pedro. The lease wouldn't be up on their apartment for, God knew, another six months! It wasn't a well-kept secret; the landlord never made refunds, and the young Foltzes were struggling.

"Madelaine, would you please do me a big, big favor? Stay in our place! It's fully furnished, and the rent's already paid. The landlord won't refund a cent when we leave." She added she'd been to the commissary, and the pantry was well stocked. "I'm leaving the icebox," she said. It was full of groceries they didn't have time to use. "Think of all those starving people in China and please, please do me a good deed ... just this once." She beamed.

She hugged Madelaine, knowing full well she'd seen plenty of starvation in the Orient. She also knew the Foltzes didn't have a red cent to their name. Every month, they were scratching just to pay the rent on a tiny flat without a stove or refrigeration, one expensive month at a time.

What the kindly soul didn't know was that God knew she had an exceptionally good heart. She could never have imagined the magnitude her acts of kindness did for a sailor's tender faith. Nor could she have known the struggles that made Harold wary and mistrustful of others in times past. That day, a compassionate friend was an instrument in the hands of Deity.

Harold was dumbfounded! "An icebox too?" That "prayer business" was the second such experience "in all [his] born days." Of course, he would never forget the miracle of getting his family home safely from China—but two extraordinary miracles? And all he had to do was ask, trust, and believe? Though he wasn't totally convinced there was a real person named God, he couldn't explain the "illogical coincidences" of speaking to Him or opening the wooden icebox and finding it full of food in their lovely, paid-for, new flat. The surest miracle that day was more than answers; it was the humbling of a sailor's heart and the tender budding of faith.

Prayer had a new convert!

Harold was convinced angels had been listening to his heartfelt desires. How else could one have known his trustful, earnest plea for help was heard? He scratched his head, trying to understand.

In the years that followed, war repeatedly called Harold Foltz to sea, to islands and shores of distant lands. But regardless of his absenteeism, frailties, and insecurities, the stranger we barely knew became the man we simply called daddy.

CHAPTER 16

Impromptu Catastrophes

A Bride in Pigtails

In the relative peace of the neighbor's cozy apartment, now their own, Harold relished the precious getting-to-know-you time spent with the woman he loved. Resting comfortably in her arms, he asked lots of questions about her life before he became part of it. He wanted to know about her family, her faith, and her friends. His curiosity was sweet and genuine. How had she come to be the person he loved so passionately? Their chance meeting, coupled with a whirlwind wedding and a slow boat to China, hardly gave them time to delve into each other's lives. There was so much to learn, so much to share of life before their impromptu meeting.

"I want to know all about you," he said.

"That's easy," she replied. "My life is pretty much an open book. I'd like to just lie here in paradise and listen to you talk. Tell me about your life before we met."

It was useful to open up and cleanse the soul. "It's not real pretty," he mumbled hesitantly. "I'll start with livin' at home on the farm …"

Harold knew better than anybody: mothering was more than birthing. But to know his life's story, one must first examine the hearts of a naïve young woman named Ruth Hunt and a staunch German named Foltz. History is replete with passionate clashes but none more unsteady than the relationship within Harold's family—between Harold and his mother.

She was mighty proud to be a fourth-generation "Reb" and reveled in talk of her forefathers' historical prominence. In revolutionary times, her patriotic ancestors planted roots in the rich, fertile soil of the South. Adventurous people of vision and wealth, they were devoted to the causes of liberty and freedom. But in the 1920s, Ruth, Harold's mother, was of a mind to swing with current trends. Her prejudices were "deeper an' more extensive than the Guff a Mexico." She boasted of descending from "slave-ownin' masters and the clan."

After the Civil War, when Johnny came marching home, hostilities should have ended, but they never did. When pressed, Ruth whispered family secrets. Her comments were never complimentary to the blue and gold.

And speaking of the top side of Harold's pedigree, he said his father's family were proud Germans, through and through. From postrevolutionary times, the family farmed contentedly in the Shenandoah and Ohio valleys.

Floyd, Harold's father, planned a future in the north, fully intending to continue his forefathers' traditions. But in the kaleidoscope of chance, young Floyd fell hopelessly in love with a pretty young southerner named Ruth Hunt. She was only fifteen—and a young one at that! He was twenty-three and should have recognized a real rebel when he kissed her. A precocious young "thang," she quickly announced life without him would be unbearable, and she refused to listen to anything she didn't want to hear! Chances were slim she would ever adjust to married life in the North, but she said Floyd was ever' thang she ever wanted. She'd "give up the moon for him—and take the South with her."

By trade, Floyd was a hardworking mechanic and managed a fair-sized family farm. He never considered home anywhere but the beautiful, fertile farmlands of Ohio. His family, pillars in the community, were longtime residents. Floyd was confident he could provide a comfortable life for a bride and future family—in the North, of course.

And so it was on a sunny afternoon, with the grandest of aspirations, the North and South declared a temporary truce as Floyd and Ruth affirmed themselves man and wife 'til death parted them.

Harold said he heard chatter from the closest of family members—his mother was rebellious and self-centered. But she was charming as her shiny, dark braids danced in the sun. They agreed she definitely belonged in the South. And oddly, the girl came from a large family and did her best to avoid responsibility.

It was on a lazy afternoon that she and Thelma, her younger sister, planned a day at the beach—fishin' (Thelma called it) without a pole.

Of course, glances between strangers were flirtatious. The young man was handsome, bathing in the sun. Ruth loved the beach and coquettishly moved her bare feet in the sand, straightened the handmade sundress, and glanced shyly at the stranger.

Thelma whispered, "He talks like a Yankee-man, a real carpetbagger. I reckon he ain't from 'round these here parts or we'd a knowed it."

Oozing southern charm, Ruth whispered, "I know he ain't no southern boy, but he's real good-lookin'."

"Ain't met many boys you don't think's good-lookin', sista' Ruth." It wasn't a well-kept secret. The girls fished for male attention as discreetly as a gator stalking lunch in the swamp.

Noting his uneasiness, Ruth turned to Thelma; aware blushes had attached themselves to her cheeks. It was evident he'd overheard their private twittering. Ruth drew her shoulders upward and giggled.

Floyd, vacationing in Florida, was just looking for a good time when he spotted the pretty girls sunbathing on the sand. From the very beginning, Ruth had a bead on him. Her usual preference, of course, was anyone south of the Mason-Dixon. On the other hand, he was partial to fun-loving German girls—that is, until he met Ruth Hunt. Setting differences aside, Ruth and Floyd felt an immediate attraction. They spent lazy afternoons and colorful sunsets together until the fire of her presence filled him with visions of happiness.

"Will ya meet me here tomorrow?" he asked. Ruth's face reddened as he held her hands.

"Sure 'nough, I will, Mr. Floyd."

Ruth was her own gritty person, accustomed to having things her way. Determined and headstrong, she was as flirty and fair as Floyd was German. Neither of them knew self-centeredness was the curse of a foolish person. Beautiful in the last rays of the sunset, Ruth looked at Floyd and smiled. He was the one, the only one she wanted, and her head was spinning. She knew full well he was a Yank, pitied him, and ignored what she didn't want to challenge. With moonlight sparkling on the sea, Ruth was busy drawing visions of her future on the insides of her eyelids.

"Tomorrow, same time, same place?" Floyd leaned onto her cheek and kissed it tenderly. "Good night, Miss Ruthy," he said.

Out of his earshot, Ruth swooned and exclaimed, "He's the most won'erful man in the whole world. I'm gonna marry him, Thelma. He's really, really special."

"Daddy ain't a-gonna let you marry nobody at fifteen, 'specially no carpetbagger."

"Well, I'm nearin' sixteen, an' I can do whatevah I want. Ain't nobody gonna stop me!"

"By the time ya all's the marryin' age, that Yankee'll be long gone with a wife and chill'in," crowed Thelma. "Besides, you ain't even growed-up yet."

"That don't matter none." Ruth pouted. "You just wait. I'm gonna be his ever-lovin' wife!"

Thelma rolled her eyes and sighed. Trying to reason with her stubborn sister was pointless. When Ruth locked her mind in place, she held the only key. Nobody knew it better than Thelma, except Ruth herself.

"I'll tell Daddy ya'll be comin' along soon." Thelma sighed again.

Floyd, proud of his Deutschland heritage, was a purebred through and through. Industrious, studious, and intelligent, he seldom stopped to smell the flowers. But a rare Floridian trip changed his life forever. Little did he envision the impulsiveness that would net future unimaginable angst.

The next evening, they met, and Ruth melted in his arms, her dark eyes flashing ardently. The heady fragrance of the night was overpowering. Was it days or weeks since their beachside meeting? "I really love you, Mr. Floyd."

In the impulsiveness of the moment, there was plenty Ruth never expected. She said she wasn't gonna live without him. Thelma said Ruth was in love with fantasy! Inexperienced with serious matters of the heart, they knew little of life, the world, or the intentions of a young man wanting a forever wife and family. It was uncharacteristic for him to rush into serious matters, as Ruth did, without defining the deeper meaning of "I do" or "I will." But Ruth, dressed in white, rushed from her sixteenth birthday party to the altar, promising to love, honor, and cherish him all the blooming days of her life!

The wedding was intimate—mainly Ruth's kin and surprised acquaintances. When the preacher said, "You may kiss the bride," it was a done deal. Well-wishers pelted the couple with rose petals and rice. Ruth waved the marriage certificate that read, "Ruth Mary Hunt, age 16, of Tampa, Florida …" Her fluttering heart said she'd always love him. She wasn't thinking ten years down the road, not even ten months.

Cotton dresses and sweaters did little to keep the summer sunshine in Ruth's new life. She'd traded a veranda in the sun for a farmhouse in the frozen fields of Ohio. She was surprised to learn her passion for home and the South was more profound than expected. And she quickly realized her southern drawl did little to garner friendships in the new neighborhood.

Why had the couple not taken time to explore their significant differences? By the time Ruth acknowledged she was a full-blooded redneck far, far from Dixie, she was a miserable, discontented wife and a sickly, expectant mother. What was it, the pungent scent of magnolias or the warmth of the soft winds off the Gulf that lulled her into thinking fire and ice could coexist? In the nakedness of an Ohio winter, Ruth struggled to adjust—not doing it very well.

On a bright, subzero night in January 1916, Ruth's infant son was born. She named him Harold, Harold William Foltz. He was as cute as the dickens, but Ruth was never as fond of the dickens as she should have been. She was homesick, off-kilter, hormonally challenged, and full of misgivings. Though Ruth wasn't ready to admit it, she was beginning to look for the back door out of responsibility. If she'd had a sledgehammer, she couldn't have done more damage to her psyche and marriage than she did. Duty had become a nasty, unwanted reality. And her small circle of foreign Midwestern relatives was suffocating.

From the beginning, the family buzz was that the marriage was a mistake. Ruth was never a happy mother. Neither she nor the baby's demands rested. Tensions and anguish clanged like cymbals. Helpful relatives encouraged her to nurse, but Ruth said she didn't "want no baby suckin' on mah tender breasts! That stuff's for nannies and wet nurses." Black nannies in the North were unheard of, but Ruth longed for one just the same. Floyd's family raised their eyebrows, glancing knowingly at one another. They knew nursing made healthy babies, even if Ruth wouldn't hear of it.

Neither of the newlyweds settled into parenthood well. Dirty diapers made Ruth nauseous. She complained the old scrubboard ruined her nails and made her hands raw. Life became a battleground, and for the record, Ruth had a bad case of PMS in perpetuity. Perhaps others thought the outside temperature made life glacial in the Foltz household, but it wasn't true. Ruth always reminded herself, and everyone else, how far she was from home, her people, and everything southern.

One day, the postman delivered a note from Thelma, and Ruth was ecstatic. It indicated she was planning a sisterly visit—to see the baby. However, when her sister arrived, Ruth's frustrations only intensified. Thelma chattered continually about the happy-go-lucky life she was living. She didn't answer to anyone but herself. Though Ruth wouldn't admit it, she was jealous. Floyd's relatives graciously entertained the Southerners, but Ruth never forgot for a moment they were Rebs. And Ruth complained, "They's Yankees, ever' bloomin' one of 'em!"

When Thelma returned home to sunny, beautiful Florida, Ruth tended the baby by herself and the endless chores associated with the life she'd chosen. But her mind wandered to carefree days with Thelma. She assumed it must have been the moonlight that blinded her. For all too soon, the holidays Ruth envisioned, motherhood and married life-to-be, were an unmitigated, lackluster existence. After an especially egregious quarrel with her husband, Ruth's tearstained, angry face said it all: "I wanna go home! This ain't livin'. I hate this place. I hate them icy winds seepin' in round them winders and doors. I hate my life, an' I'm sick a you, Floyd Foltz! Why'd you move me to this awful place? I don't belong here. You're responsible for that baby, not me. You can keep it! I nevah wanted no kids anyway an' I ain't nevah gonna be no wet nurse to nobody. An' furthermore, I ain't a-gonna be no slave to you!"

Her whiney, constant irritability was destroying Floyd's zest for life. He felt like a willow in a hurricane, bending this way and that, trying insufferably to please her. He could fix drafts in the house, but there was no fixing the widening cracks in their relationship. Ruth despised nearly everything he felt was important.

A mirror-loving woman, she dreamed of becoming a respectable lady of fashion and society, envisioning herself sporting the latest trends. Someday, her tidy closet would be packed with night-clubbing garb, boxes of trendy shoes, and fancy chapeaus. She'd cinch in her already tiny waist and nibble to maintain a silhouette all southern bells coveted. Partying and flapping, she envisioned piles of pearls dangling and bouncing from her long, pretty neck.

Floyd interrupted her daydreams: "Ruth, honey, we gotta stop this nonsense. We got a family that needs us. Can't you try to find some peace with me and the little guy? Spring's a-comin'. You'll see how beautiful and green the fields will be and how hot the valley is in July." He promised when winter came again, they'd vacation in Florida if that's what she really wanted. He did his best to amuse her with stories of fireflies that twinkled and blinked on sweltering summer evenings. He promised she'd wish for some of those cool breezes when summer arrived. He smiled and asked her to be patient, to have hope for brighter tomorrows. He'd try harder to make her happy. He begged her to be kinder to the baby.

"Nev'ah," she replied coldly.

As if he hadn't heard her, Floyd continued, "We'll churn ice cream on the front porch and feed some to little Harold. He'll be teething by then."

When the ice cream melted, Harold had a baby brother. They named him Jon after Ruth's favorite sibling, living the good life down south. Unwaning despondency reminded Ruth how much she missed her *real* family and the lightheartedness of adolescence. At twenty, Ruth felt old as she preened the young face in the looking glass.

Like Harold, the new infant had healthy lungs. Ruth wasn't amused. Passing the tiny crib, she looked at the baby with aversion. She told Floyd she didn't want any babies, and now she had two!

"Floyd, you did this to me," she whined.

As promised, summer, with its proliferation of flowers and bees, came and went. And in the fall, Annie, Floyd's long-suffering mother, taught Ruth to make delicious sauerkraut. They stored it in large crocks in the basement. Ruth hated the smelly stuff! They bottled berry jam, peaches, pickles, and cherries, laying in supplies for winter. Throughout the steamy, one-on-one visits, Annie hoped to reason with her hapless kin. As she assisted Ruth in honing unwanted skills, the ladies suffered heart-to-heart chats. They spoke of serious riffs affecting them all. Ruth had plenty to say but suffered from selective listening. She didn't want any talking about the good life or better ways of mothering.

"I know it's a lot of responsibility, child. Floyd's a good man. He works hard to give you a good life. Those little boys need you, and Floyd's providin' a nice place to raise 'em. Growin' up, takin' on responsibilities of a family can be wearisome. But a home, those little kids—that's women's work. You'll get used to it and learn to enjoy it," she said. "Good old-fashioned toilin' is part a life, Ruthy ..."

The news wasn't news. If Ruth even heard her thoughtful mother-in-law, she didn't believe a word of it. Worrying left new wrinkles and grayer hair on the portly, deeply concerned woman. Ruth's malcontent was blatantly obvious, and a lack of integrity damned Ruth's desire to move forward. Though she was young and attractive with a home of her own, a faithful husband, and two rambunctious sons, restlessness nipped at Ruth like a swarm of pesky mosquitoes. Who said family life was ever a woman's dream? Ruth never dreamt of household chores or squally kids. Smelly diapers made her nauseous. Cooking for a tired man, mopping floors over and over, dragging toddlers wherever she went— the unwanted anchors were getting heavier by the month. Even the Yankee grocer annoyed her. He didn't stock okra or grits!

Farming and machine shop talk bored Ruth to tears. She bellyached and daydreamed of the revelry she was missing—the bliss Thelma wasn't. Thel's carefree letters didn't help. She gushed over a bevy of ever-changing beaux, social events, and the pleasures of single life. She confessed she'd grown to like the speakeasies and hooch they served. Unwittingly, Thelma was salting Ruth's sores of pettiness. The kids bawled for her attention as Ruth fantasized about the good ole carefree southern hospitality she was missing. She grumbled that she couldn't stand much more. Each time the postman delivered another letter, Ruth blubbered anew and cursed her misfortune.

It shouldn't have surprised anyone, but Floyd was irritated and very quick-tempered. He expected his wife to share responsibilities. Coming home to a grumbling shrew was worse than not coming home at all. His absence gave Ruth longer days and nights to stew. She made "his weaknesses," as she called them, excuses for her tantrums as she egged him into fights. It wasn't hard to get his goat—not hard at all. When the man finally exploded, he justified her dissatisfaction. If he'd hit her (and ofttimes he felt she deserved it), she'd have proof of his meanness—but he never did. But it was easier to taunt him into a Sea of Wrath than to appease the beast of fury she created. When she wasn't yapping, she gritted her teeth and muttered epithets under her breath.

"Why can't you pick up a broom and do some sweepin'?" she nagged. "Them kids keep droppin' thangs on mah clean floors, puttin' their dirty hands all over them shiny winders. It nevah stops! I can't stand doin' the same thangs over an' over. I don't know how much more of this I can stand. I hate it! All of it."

Floyd clenched his jaw. He was tired and often worked the night shift to help with the responsibilities of two small sons. But the squabbles rarely ceased—just one nasty blow after another. His temper far outran his mouth. He was upset and frustrated with her carping and snarled like a mad dog. Hell-bent, out of control, he often took his frustrations out on his kids and whooped 'em good! The youngins cried for safety that fell on deaf ears. Living in a war zone was taking its toll on the appallingly dysfunctional family.

"Oh, honey! I had no idea your family faced such terrible times," Madelaine said.

Harold sighed and wistfully replied, "Well, I don't get into those awful times very often. But since you asked, I've only told you the better part of being a kid. I guess it was harder on Jonny than for me. He was just a sensitive little guy, and I—I was his big brother, trying to do the best I could."

She kissed the tears that rolled freely down his cheeks—an emotion only she ever saw. "We have each other now," she consoled gently, "and a future of bright tomorrows. I'll take care of and love you forever. Those awful days are behind us. Let's say our evening prayers and rest through the night. We have plenty for which to be thankful."

CHAPTER 17

The Easy Way Out

Findlay, Ohio, 1926, Hal's Hometown

Madelaine's love was sensitive to matters of the heart—and she was fine-tuned to his. Harold was sullen and massively disturbed. It was easy to tell the wounds from the simple question about his past were still unhealed. He thought he could rattle off his childhood history and move on, but it wasn't that simple.

"Honey, if there's more about the past that's still bothering you, we can get it out in the open if you want. Or we can leave it brewing. But if the thoughts are still nagging at you, if there are things that need to be washed away like old rags, and time isn't doing the job, we can talk whenever you want to. Perhaps discussing things that are still troubling will help close the book, and we can move on without the pain." It wasn't pretty, but it was the truth.

"I think you should know the rest of the story," he mumbled, "and perhaps it won't hurt so much. Me and Jon have never been able to figure out why … she didn't want us."

Madelaine kissed him on the cheek and said, "The baby's still sleeping, and I'm always ready to listen if you're ready to talk."

"I know where ugly begins," Harold said. "I'm just not sure where it ends. We were livin' in a war zone, Jon and me. I remember crying, 'Daddy, Daddy, don't hit me no more. I'm sorry. I'll never ever do it again.'"

He had no idea what he was sorry for, but he said it anyway. Little Jon crawled into a corner, shook his hands in the air, and wailed. What had they done to cause the ear-splitting matches? Floyd was perpetually angry. He raged at perceived disobediences, infractions of unwritten laws, and blamed the kids for Ruth's resentment and deepening dissatisfaction.

"Grow up!" Floyd screamed at her. His out-of-control antagonism added fodder to Ruth's enlarging arsenal of reasons for change. He was dictatorial. Was she the only one who saw the fire in his eyes and felt the wrath of his touch? With cause, she was fearful and wondered why nobody but her seemed to know Floyd had a dangerous, vicious temper—the Foltz temper, they called it. By the following winter, no firewood amount could soften the deadlock that raged between Ruth and Floyd.

One wretched afternoon, hell-bent on solving her most pressing issues, Ruth bundled the children in a couple of warm sweaters and grabbed a woolly blanket. She packed them like sacks of potatoes, trudging through the mud to the waiting automobile.

"Where are we going, Mommy?"

She didn't answer, nor did she glance at the rearview mirror into their questioning eyes. Curious, they waited for answers that didn't come. Her sons, ages three and five, asked more questions. Ruth's frigid nonresponse was not unusual, but it was always upsetting. Harold, ever Jon's protector, did his best to console his little brother shivering in the back seat of the old car. They chattered quietly, sadly to each other.

"Mommy's busy," Harold whispered.

"Tell me a sto-ey," replied little Jon.

Harold tucked the blanket around him and said he couldn't think of any stories, but he sang their favorite song, "Three Blind Mice." Jon giggled and tried to repeat the strange lyrics. "She cut off their tails with a carving knife ..." Ruth gripped the steering wheel tighter and stared straight ahead through the steamy windshield. She was in no mood for kids or tailless rodents.

Defiantly, with true grit, she sped to a large old house on the outskirts of the city. The children strained, peering through the icy window at the unfriendly looking structure. That the large house ahead of them needed a coat of paint was the least of their worries. Large trees hovered high above the dilapidated porch. Bleak and barren, they were dusted with snow. Even if the trees sported summer leaves, the limbs were too old and too high for climbing or children's swings.

Ruth stopped the car, half turned toward the back seat, and unemotionally announced, "The people in that big, roomy house are gonna take good care of y'all!"

Her incessantly flat voice was filled with resilience. Here, she thought, was the solution for all of her troubles: dump the kids and get outta town—way out. Matter-of-factly, she told the whimpering, panicking brood she was going away and they couldn't go with her.

"Don't leave us, Mommy. Please don't leave us here. We'll be good. We promise, promise forever—please don't go!" Harold leaped from his seat and reached for his glacial mother, but she leaned forward, out of reach, and shrugged her shoulders.

At twenty-two, Ruth was sure her life was a total waste. She'd given Floyd her best, she thought—five long years. Harold sensed her unspoken thoughts. She didn't want him. But he loved her and needed her. He wailed brokenheartedly, not to further torment her but because the pain in his soul was inconsolable. Little Jon, too young to comprehend the severity of her intent, simply howled and shook with fear.

"Mommy, Mommy, I need you," he sobbed.

Ruth said her peace and rested her head on the steering wheel. She didn't want to argue or debate. She wasn't really leaving them alone. Those fine people in the orphanage/boardinghouse knew what to do with a couple of nice little boys. She didn't—nor did she want to know. Surely someone would give them a nice home. Floyd didn't have to know, at least not from her lips.

When Ruth lost her nerve and accepted the fact that she couldn't drag the kids to the door, a wave of unexpected grief covered her like a sudden hailstorm. She grabbed a dainty white linen hanky from her purse and blew her runny nose. Then she dabbed at the annoying tears. The darn things ran hotly down her cheeks and made her even madder. In a sudden burst of rage, she hammered on the steering wheel, livid with herself, and gave in.

Resigned to her fate, she dropped her shaking hands onto her lap and tried not to feel the weight of responsibility. Sighing, she begrudgingly found the strength to turn the key and push the starter button. The engine moaned until it turned over. She grabbed the large black steering wheel with both hands and stepped on the gas. Gravel flew into the air as she made a U-turn in the driveway. She didn't even look for oncoming cars as she pulled onto the slippery main road. Deep in thought, she steered the sedan in silence. Harold and Jon, frightened and confused, scarcely dared to breathe.

Ruth had finally made up her mind. They could stay, but she would not. She told herself Floyd was responsible for the kids; he could figure out what to do with them. She reasoned she'd go crazy if she hung on much longer. Shuddering, she imagined years and years of growing old and wrinkled, living in that Godforsaken Yankee land, existing with a man she loathed. It was sapping the life right out of her. She told herself, again and again, she "nevah wanted the job in the first place or the chillin'."

Considering her alternative options made Ruth's head swim, but she thought of little else. She asked herself how long she should be traveling on the wrong road of life before turning around, heading for a new tomorrow—starting over with a clean slate. It was amazing how easily she justified herself. What else could she do to divest herself of a life that was making her miserable? It would have been cruel to turn the kids out into the snow, but more than once, it crossed her mind.

With the decision behind her not to leave her kids at the orphanage, Ruth was confident she could hand them over to Floyd's family. They were good ole Yanks, and she was ready to wave the white flag.

Thelma's frequent letters encouraged her sister to move on. Perhaps she meant for Ruth to bring the kids and visit for a spell. But Ruth interpreted the words as an invitation to start over. She was already mentally packing for home. And there wasn't any room in her plans for a couple of needy kids, not even her own.

The rhythm of the windshield wipers was hypnotic. Ruth tried hard not to think at all, just drive. She steered mindlessly until, at last, she spotted the whitewashed mailbox with FOLTZ scribbled on it. It was as if the automobile knew the way home by itself. The car gently rocked as she turned onto the muddy, rutted driveway. At the end of the road, Ruth turned off the engine. She momentarily rested her weary head on the steering wheel and sat quietly. No one moved.

Resigned, she took a deep breath, opened the door, and packed the kids into the tidy, unfriendly house. Harold stared at his mother with large, brown, innocent eyes. Bravely, he asked, "What are you doin', Mommy?"

His childlike question should have pricked her conscience, but it didn't. Curious and fearful, the trembling children stood in the doorway of her bedroom and watched as Ruth methodically filled her suitcases. Jonny sucked his thumb, and Harold did his best to stay out of her way.

"Where we goin', Mommy?" Harold asked.

Ruth didn't answer. She moved about the room as though the children were invisible. When her bags were packed, Ruth struggled to the car with them. Only then did she announce, "Yo father'll be here soon. He'll take care of you. Mind your Ps and Qs, ya hear? And don't make yo' daddy mad. Be good little boys. Y'all hear me?"

Ruth told herself she really didn't care. Then, on second thought, she turned to the pale, open-mouthed children and announced, "Harold, you're the little man of the house now. Y'all take good care of your little brother."

Harold stood in the open doorway, holding a woolen blanket. He watched his mother get into the car and slam the door. Haphazardly, she patted the bulging bags in the back seat and flipped off the switch of accountability. She never looked back.

Tears streamed down Harold's soft, round face. He thought of chasing after her, but little Jon couldn't run very fast. Besides, Jonny's teeth were chattering. Stuffing grief somewhere deep inside, Harold draped the blanket around his little brother's shoulders and dutifully comforted him. "Don't you worry none. I'm takin' good care of ya, like Mama said."

Harold closed the heavy door and wiped his runny nose on his sleeve. He helped Jonny climb onto the horsehair sofa, sat beside him, and stared through the spotless window until the black car disappeared.

Remembering his mother's final words, Harold hugged little Jonny even closer. Crushed, lonely, and confused, they wept bitterly.

If Ruth had looked in the rearview mirror, she would have seen the lace curtain draped to the side of the sofa and two little faces peering painfully at desertion. But at the end of the driveway, she sped southward, convinced it was the right thing to do. After all, she deserved a better life.

At last, she was free.

"They'll get over it," she told herself. "They're young. They'll forget." But they never ever did.

Married life was never what Ruth envisioned. Obsessed with the looking glass, she was positive new wrinkles were prematurely attaching themselves to her face. She was only twenty-two, but it felt like ninety. She told herself living with Yankees, the hasty marriage, and unwanted kids were all big mistakes—and wondered if she should have left sooner. But she stuck it out five long, complaining, cantankerous years, cringing at the loss of her youth. When she slammed the door behind her, Ruth didn't even notice, nor would she have bothered to straighten, the plaque on the wall that fortuitously read, LOVE AT HOME.

"Don't wait up for me, y'all hear," she said, "cuz I ain't nev'ah comin' back!"

Sadly, it was the only promise to her family she ever kept.

CHAPTER 18

Pals Forever

He Ain't Heavy ... He's My Brother

Of course, Floyd couldn't manage his own life and raise a couple of rambunctious, deserted youngsters by himself. He was unprepared and felt empty—barely able to reconstruct his own shattered world. Disillusioned and confused, the angry father became every child's nightmare—frustrated, rage filled, and brutal. When he met and married another young thing, she promised to ease his burdens. He hoped he'd found a forever companion and stepmother for his kids. But, as an only child, she never wanted children in the first place and, unfortunately, parented even more miserably than Floyd.

No one claimed responsibility for finally reporting the mistreatment of the children to the civil authorities, nor was the informant ever acknowledged. It would have been a massive breach of confidentiality, but the truth came out in court. The final documents listed the two minor children as wards of the court.

Annie, Floyd's saintly mother, filled with compassion, stepped forward and pleaded for custody of the confused, battered little boys. They were her grandsons, and she loved them. Old, widowed, and experienced, she knew what it meant to be a mother—and a loving grandmother. If anyone could breach the hemorrhages in the children's hearts, it was her.

"Granted, effective immediately," ordered the white-haired judge.

Grandma Foltz was a dear, jolly soul, filled with hugs and kindness. Under her wings, the youngsters learned valuable lessons of gratitude, acceptance, and unconditional love. She promised security and warmth and delivered an abundance of home-baked cookies and love. Smiling, she told Harold, "You can be my helper. The water bucket seems heavier than it used to be. Would you carry it to the house for me, son?"

"Me too, Grandma! I can help," said little Jon. Small and skinny for his age, his big blue eyes pleaded for love. He needed to be needed.

"There's plenty of work for all of us," Grandma said. "I'm going to need helpers to eat all these delicious apple pies and fresh carrots and tomatoes from the garden!"

Harold felt guilty. He wasn't sure why he felt that way, but he did. The two of them should not be her responsibility. He knew they were burdensome, even if she said they weren't.

Minding his mother's last words, Harold told Jon not to worry; he would forever take care of him. But at night, in the loneliness and silence of their attic bedroom, the brothers wept quietly in the dark. Harold was only ten years old, but he vowed as soon as he could, he was going to make his own way in life. He told Jon he would always be there for him, and he'd never let anyone hurt either of them again, ever.

"Me and you, we're pals forever, Jon."

Pulling the covers tightly over themselves, Harold promised one day they'd go to Florida and find their mother. It was the children's private talk, of course—the kind Grandma wouldn't have wanted to hear.

"Do you think Mommy will even know us? I heared she don't want us no more," said the eight-year-old.

Harold bristled and whispered, "Ah, that's just people talk. She'll get a kick outta seeing me and you all growed up."

Jon was pensive. "What's it like in Florida?"

Though he'd never been anywhere, Harold told him about the gulf, the gators, and the deep blue sea. He'd been studying his geography book in school. Anything to do with the South, with Florida in particular, captured his interest. "It's a place we're gonna like when we get there 'cause it's nice and warm all the time. It never snows where Mom is. She hates snow. You'll like it, I promise," said Harold.

"When?" Jon asked excitedly.

"Ahh, I dunno. Someday. We gotta get growed-up first."

With so many unanswered adult questions about life and desertion, the boys found it difficult to believe in things not seen and hardly felt. Insecurity had a perceptible hold on Jon's heart, and his wounds seemed bottomless. Rejection and bewilderment were painful, but the boys bottled their feelings, waiting for a day the sorrow would disappear. And so the codependent youths relied upon each other and their grandmother for answers too grandiose for any of them to comprehend.

The antique pump organ in Grandma's parlor helped with the transition. Ofttimes, she entertained her charges with music. They laughed as she wore herself out, alternately pumping the pedals on the floor until her entire body swayed from side to side. Occasionally, the little guys placed themselves on either side of the pedals and took turns pumping in rhythm as she played. Their favorite song, of course, was "Three Blind Mice." As she played it repeatedly, they created a form of harmony. Over and over, the three of them clapped and laughed, sometimes imitating the mice that scurried away and hid in the closet.

Annie was a Godly woman. She bought junior-sized Sunday clothes, and on the Sabbath, she proudly took her grandsons to church. Though the boys were respectful and attentive, they found the church talk confusing. The children were ill at ease when it came to warming up to strangers. Jon held his brother's arm and did his best to hide behind his ten-year-old protector. When the chatter softened, parishioners took their seats in the homey chapel. To keep an eye on her boys, Annie proudly parked them in the first row. Then, winking and raising one eyebrow, she took her place on the organ bench, waiting for services to begin and end.

In the evenings, Grandma read Bible stories and knelt with the children at bedtime. She said they needed to pray for their father and mother. Wide-eyed, the boys stared at her and repeated her words in the dark. Concluding, she tucked them into bed and attempted to answer nagging questions: Does God know our mamma moved away to Florida? Does He know we live here with you, Grandma Annie? Does He know our daddy doesn't love us anymore?

She gave Jon an extra hug. Her heart ached for them—though she never said a bad word about her son's choice of wives. Annie often bit her lip, changed the subject, or soothed the situation with a cookie or two.

In his teenage years, Harold shoveled snowy walkways in the bitter winter months, split firewood for the house, and walked to school with Jon. He was glad to be earning his dough by helping the neighbors and his elderly grandmother. He worked in the cold until his ears were red, his face was white, and his fingertips blue. Grandmother said that, like the rest of her relatives, she was a proud and active Democrat.

At fifteen, Harold was doing his best to save enough money for a trip to the South. Frugal, he had conceptualized goals and needed all the money he could earn. Impressed with his ambition, the neighbors paid him with icy coins and warm appreciation. They knew he was dependable and always willing to lend a helping hand. Little did they know he loathed the frigid conditions and vowed someday to give it all up and move to a warmer climate.

"Your dad used to shovel for us when he was about your age," volunteered a satisfied neighbor. "When them pointy icicles on the porch was a meltin', he snapped 'em off and sucked on 'em like they was candy." Harold's smile dropped. He didn't like the comparison between himself and his father.

"Well, I best be goin'," replied the red-cheeked boy. "It's gettin' late, and I gotta help my brother with his schoolwork."

Grandma told Harold to wrap himself in a blanket and sit next to the toasty coal stove. She brought him a cup of hot cider and breathed in the smell of fall. Shivering, he warmed his cold hands on the hot mug.

"How much you earnin'?" Jon inquired.

Harold reached into his pocket and rolled the silver coins in his fingers. "Oh, I'm gettin' lots of dough. It ain't enough yet, but my sock's gettin' pretty heavy."

He was an adolescent with a mission, and his daydreams were maturing. One day, he overheard his grandmother talking about family in Florida. He honed in on the conversation and asked questions she didn't want to answer. She confessed she had a phone number where she thought his mother could be reached. Late into the night, Harold wondered if he had the nerve to make the call. He contemplated what he'd say, what she'd say.

"Long distance," droned the operator. "I have your party on the line. Go ahead, sir ..."

The conversation was awkward. Stammering and trying his best to sound like a man, he muttered, "Harold. It's Harold, your son, Mom. I, uh, I wanna come to see you."

Annie held her breath and watched as the blood seeped from his face.

"I can? When?"

"Lemme talk to her!" Jon squealed.

"It's me, Mommy. Jon, your other son. Remember me? Can I come and see you too? I wanna go to Florida with Harold. I wanna live there with you and ..."

Ruth's response to the unexpected call was cold. The truth was she didn't have anything to say. Her tactlessness was painful and more profound than razor cuts. Of course, she missed them, she said, and loved them, but her time was, uh, occupied. Unwittingly, the conversations gave the boys a spark of optimism, an air balloon of possibilities. Though she hadn't meant to, Ruth fostered a fantasy of options. Truth be known, it was more like a Hindenburg of Hope. Anticipating a ride to happiness, Ruth's sons, still gullible in their youth, climbed aboard.

Harold's sock was sufficiently filling with enough money for a bus ticket. Hoping her aloofness meant she indeed was busy, the boys were excited just to have heard her voice. Though she hadn't seen her sons in years, Harold trembled, hoping she'd be smiling when he arrived. If she didn't recognize him, he assured her he could pick her out of any crowd. The family said they strongly resembled each other with dark brown hair and eyes.

Stretching out on his bed, Harold folded his arms behind his head and pondered. He tried to unravel adult feelings he was incapable of understanding. Deep in thought, his eyes scanned the room and fell upon a photograph. It was his mother, cuddling a chubby baby, her firstborn. His heart skipped a beat. So many years had passed. Indeed, she'd be smiling again, waiting to greet him with love, calling his name when he arrived in Florida. If she'd missed him only half as much as he'd missed her ... He allowed his mind to wander.

Harold took a piece of blue-lined paper from his school folder and followed up his phone call with a letter. Grandma knew Ruth's address but was worried about even more profound disappointments. She knew her former daughter-in-law a lot better than did her grandson. She told Harold there was a possibility he could be disappointed. Harold finished his short letter and mailed it; he said he'd call her when he arrived in Tampa. But she never wrote back. Busy, he thought.

After hearing the voice he had not heard for years, Jon was hopping with joy until his big brother announced he was traveling alone. Jon's jaw dropped in stunned disbelief. "What do you mean you're travelin' alone?"

"You gotta finish your schoolin'," Harold replied. "I'm goin' to Florida by myself 'cause that's all the dough I got. I'll send for you as soon as I earn the rest of the money for your ticket. I'm gonna go to work and save every cent for you."

"You ain't finished with your schoolin' neither, Harold!" Jon scowled momentarily, until his face gave way to grief. "You can't leave me! What would I do without you? We've always been together, me and you. I'm goin', and you can't stop me!"

High pitched and resolute, he whimpered again, "I'm goin' with you!" Harold took his little brother by the shoulders and promised he'd send for him as soon as he earned the needed money, and he held his ground. Though he'd done his best to reassure the thirteen-year-old their lives were going to be better, Jon shuddered. He'd never been separated from his best friend, and just the thought of it broke his heart.

Inconsolably, he said, "Me and you. We're goin' together—right, Harold? You ain't really leavin' me, are ya? What would I do without you? You're all I got in the whole world! You can't leave me. I can get a job, just like you. Me and you, we can work together and earn a lotta dough. I don't cost much. Whatever you're gonna do, I can do it too. Look how strong I'm getting." He flexed his skinny arms for Harold to admire. "See? I told you. I'm gettin' stronger every day!"

"You gotta stay in school and get good grades, Jon. I don't have no place to go yet. When I get to Florida, I'll find some place for us to live.

Rusty Anchors

You gotta be patient. Wait 'til I get enough dough. I promise I'll get you. Grandma won't let nobody hurt you. You know that. I promise, double cross my heart, I'm gonna get you with me as soon as I can. But I gotta get a job first—and more dough."

He hoped his promises would ease Jon's sobbing, but they didn't. Harold stood on one foot and then the other, rubbing his head with both hands and sighing. It's tough to be strong when your best friend is sniveling. "Don't look at me that way. I said I'm comin' back for you, and I will. Promise, promise, I will."

"You're all I got in the whole world, Harold. Please don't leave me."

Harold said he had a plan. He didn't exactly know what it was yet, but he had one. He was sure their mother would love her sons when she saw them—wouldn't she? They weren't babies any longer. She'd find time for them in her busy schedule, wouldn't she? That's all they wanted, a little of her time and some loving.

"You do good in school, and we'll be at the seashore, rompin' in the sunshine before you know it. We're pals forever, Jon!"

In the morning, Harold finished his packing. A cardboard box held all he had—a couple of sweaters, his Sunday best, and a few personal things. A snapshot of himself and Jon went in last. He was saving it for his mother. She'd like a photograph of her two tall, thin sons standing in the snow, pretending to be happy. They were fine young men—wholesome and hardworking. Smiling to himself, he imagined she'd be full of pride. Eleven long years had passed since she'd left Ohio. If he wished hard enough, she'd remember the good ole times and appreciate her kids—wouldn't she?

Arthritis and age were wearing on Grandma, but she drove the boys to the bus station on Saturday morning. She never stood in Harold's way. When reasoning failed, she stepped aside and respected his decisions. Though she was convinced gross disappointments awaited him, she hoped she'd given him the strength and courage he'd surely need to face it.

Clouds of white exhaust curled around the idling bus. The rumble of the engine was exhilarating and at the same time frightening. As Grandma hugged him tightly, tears coursed down his face. He just couldn't help it. Tenderly, the brothers waved goodbye. It tore Harold's heart to see Jon so upset, but the separation was only temporary, he told himself. Jon was his responsibility, and he'd always shouldered it well. "Things are gonna be swell, Jon. Trust me. I'm gonna getchu with me before you even have time to know I'm visitin' Mom down there. Take good care of Grandma. She needs you."

"I'll be missing you real bad, Harold. Please don't forget me," Jon mumbled.

From the bus, Harold choked on his own words. Mustering confidence, he replied, "Okey dokey. You be good and mind what Grandma says. I'll be seein' ya as soon as I can—and I'll be writin' to ya. You do good in school 'cause you're smarter than me, and I know you're gonna need first-rate grades to get a good job someday. Do your schoolwork every night and look for my letters. I love ya, Jon. Write back, 'cause I'm already missin' ya."

Traveling on faith, Harold was confident he could make a better life for himself and Jon. Waving again, he tried to smile. Then, through the steamy window, he looked directly at his brother and mouthed his silent promise: "We're gonna get a place to live in Florida, me and you. I'm comin' back for you. I double swear it—you and me, pals forever. Forever …"

CHAPTER 19

Uncle Sam's Son

Florida, 1932

It was frigid when Harold reached the coast of Florida. Oh, it wasn't the ambient temperature; it was the reception. As weary passengers filed off the bus, greeted by friends and family, he stood alone in the thinning crowd. He'd been worrying since he left Jon at the depot, but he kept it to himself, of course. Would his mother even recognize him? It was his fondest expectation that she would. The empty bus left a small cloud of smoke as it exited the terminal.

She wasn't there.

Harold was devastated and afraid. He pulled a small slip of paper from his pocket and reread the telephone number. Taking the information with him was proving to be a wisely heeded prompting. He shuffled into the terminal and asked to use the telephone. He and a clerk were the only two people in the large, deserted station. He said his mother must have forgotten this was the day he was arriving. "Sure," replied the friendly clerk. "The tella-fon's over tha' in na corner."

When dialed, the phone rang and rang—but Ruth wasn't home, so he seated himself on a wooden bench and waited, and waited, and waited.

It was after dark when a tall, thin lady rushed to the door of the nearly empty room and asked the clerk if she'd seen a young man from—and there he was, alone and waiting.

"Why, I reckon you mus' be Harold. Are ya?"

She identified herself as Aunt Thelma and made some flimsy excuses for her hairbrained sister's forgetfulness. "Nev'ah ya mind a thang." She smiled. "I'm takin' ya to my place, an' we'll work thangs out tomarra."

Thelma had a great little business in a shop downtown. She'd made a living space for herself in the back and called it home—a toilet, hotplate, and a small bed. It was tidy enough but cramped. Chattering incessantly about nothing, Thelma located a cot and blanket and told Harold he was welcome to stay as long as he wanted. The truth was he wasn't planning to stay at her place at all. Thelma continued, "As ya can see, I make silk neckties for gentlemen and sell 'em right here in my shop! After school, I can teach ya to make 'em, an' we'll sell yours right alongside mine." She smiled. He had so many unanswered questions—so much uncertainty.

It was several weeks before Ruth finally showed up at the tie shop. She was looking for her sister and didn't recognize her own son until he called her Mom. She could have been addressing a wooden Indian in a cigar shop for all the warmth she exuded. She said she was glad Thelma had so much extra room for him and said she'd come back another time when they weren't so busy. And when she left, Harold and Thelma looked at each other in disbelief.

"Well, son," Thelma finally said, "I guess we best be lookin' at the school nearby and get you on them rolls. Ya gotta lotta book learnin' to do. We'll get ya signed up tomorra." And she did.

Between long walks to and from school and cutting the silk ties on the bias, Harold managed to meet a few young friends his age. Their lives were far different from his, and he wasn't eager to disclose details about himself; the fewer, the better. The truth be known, Harold wasn't much interested in book learning at all and began skipping school days at a time. Soon, his grades reflected the absenteeism. He told the principal he was busy working in the tie shop; his aunt needed his help. He volunteered the fact he'd recently interviewed for another job—a second one—caddying at the golf course. Most likely, he would not be attending classes much longer. He appreciated their interest in his education, but he didn't have time for work and any more formal education. Harold, unfortunately, was only fourteen when he dropped out of school.

The manager of the private club was tall and tanned, a close friend of Aunt Thelma. He appreciated Harold's enthusiasm for work. Though he knew nothing of the game of golf, Harold was a fast learner and caddied exceptionally well—the manager's first choice. Few knew Harold was saving all of his tips in his sock—saving for Jon's trip south. Soon, his bankroll would add up to something. He put in long hours from early morning until after dark without ever complaining.

It didn't take long for him to accumulate a bevy of golfing businessmen who became good friends as well as generous benefactors. Over lunch, talking among themselves, the men made a generous offer: all expenses paid to a private university if Harold chose to further his education. They all agreed it was a splendid idea—none of them knowing Jon was waiting, expecting his big brother to keep his word. Harold appreciated the unexpected generosity. He listened intently to tales of future wealth and entitlement. They promised a life he could hardly comprehend, if only he would continue his education and dedicate himself to a better future. Harold lacked confidence in himself. He'd heard nobody wanted him too many times; he was a troublemaker—a stupid one at that! Shockingly, he declined the heady offer. As a school dropout, he was sure he'd disappoint his benefactors and waste their money. No, he planned to reunite with Jon and help him finish his education.

When Harold's sock was heavy enough, Jon arrived on a tired bus from the Midwest. His big brother greeted him happily with hugs and smiles and introduced him to their kindly aunt Thelma. Living quarters at the back of the tie shop were enlarged, and a new tie maker joined the team—working and chattering when his homework was completed. Jon worked hard, stayed in school, and achieved high marks. He didn't want to let anybody down.

Ruth made occasional visits to Thelma's shop and met her two fine sons. They had learned well how to handle disappointments and misunderstandings. After all, brothers are brothers forever, aren't they? And mothers, well, there are mothers, and then there are mothers!

As luck would have it, Harold passed a recruiting office on the way to the club. At first, he only glanced at the window. But as time passed, he began to wonder what kind of life the navy might offer.

Finally, out of curiosity, he stopped to discuss the matter with a cordial recruiter in a snappy uniform. "Join the navy and see the world!" the sailor told him, pointing to a large sign on the wall. The message resonated, and Harold said he'd think seriously about it. He reasoned, if he were gone, Aunt Thelma's backroom would be less crowded, and he could help pay for Jon's support and keep him in school. Though Harold didn't have time to educate himself, in his gut, he knew schooling was important.

He was only seventeen when Harold excitedly signed on the dotted line. By month's end, he'd be eighteen—with a bright future of travel and excitement awaiting him. Harold seemed to think the military was what he wanted for a career. It offered a reasonable salary, food on the table, and an opportunity to see the world. The more he thought about it, the more convinced he became, confident the sea was calling. With faith and trepidation resting on his shoulders, Harold officially signed the recruitment adoption papers and became the newest, real-live son of Uncle Sam. Though his future seemed opaque, he pondered his options thoughtfully and concluded the navy was his best bet.

Of course, he had no idea what the future held—or where—but then, do any of us?

CHAPTER 20

One Enchanted Evening

Columbia River, Portland, Oregon, 1938

Learning to be respectful navy style, stand at attention, salute, and always answer, "Yes, sir," wasn't difficult for the new recruit. Harold fell right in line—grateful that Jonny was doing well, spending a little time with their mother occasionally, and excelling with his studies.

Harold was surprised to receive a letter from Jon that stated their mother was getting hitched again. Grandma Annie's correspondence, always cheerful, full of gratitude for the blessings of life, ignored the news about another father for her grandsons. She praised both boys for their courage and devotion to each other. She said she knew they would excel in their chosen professions because they were good people weathering the storms of life with faith in themselves and tomorrow.

When Jonny finished the courses he was taking outside of high school, he was seriously thinking of joining the military like his big brother. The Coast Guard seemed most appealing. Until then, working in the tie shop paid for his room and board. His grades were well above average. Though he was social and a good-looking young man, he dedicated most of his time to planning and dreaming of the future.

Harold's letter stated he was being assigned to a navy hospital ship—USS *Comfort*—but he wouldn't be wearing doctor whites. He said most of the time he was covered with soot from the boilers that powered the ship. Harold said he didn't mind. He was seeing lots of new places, learning stuff to better serve Uncle Sam, and best of all, getting paid a lotta dough! He liked the respect he was receiving and not having to worry about where he'd be sleeping or eating the next day. Soon after, he wrote about his transfer to the USS *Relief*, another hospital ship.

Tying up in the mighty Columbia River and at the port in Bremerton, Washington, was a completely new experience for the young sailor. He'd never been to the Northwest, and lo and behold, the captain was planning a party! Harold reckoned it didn't get any better than that. The open house was a way of acquainting the community with the finest navy in the world, the one they were supporting. The captain invited the entire city to attend! In his letter, Harold enclosed a newspaper clipping with the announcement.

"Gee, pal," Harold wrote, "I sure wish you could be here for the big shindig! We're expectin' hundreds of the best-lookin' dames in town! I'm polishin' up my dancin' shoes." For many of the young men away from home for the first time, the newspaper article all but said, "Fair, attractive, and brave young ladies of the community are encouraged to attend."

From Madelaine's journal, she wrote the following from her perspective:

> One wonderfully, enchanted evening, the skipper of a Navy ship dropped anchor in the Columbia—not far from our home. He invited the community to an open house and tour of his meticulous vessel. I wasn't interested in the activities, but Arlaine had a bee in her bonnet. She was certain the formal, public invitation had her personal name all over it.

Arlaine, Madelaine's younger sister, was a pistol always cocked and ready to shoot (with or without provocation). She envisioned her own name at the top of the party list written in bold letters! Without hesitation, she made serious plans to attend the party. Visions of pretty dresses and an upswept hairdo waltzed through her mind. Though she already knew her conservative parents' reaction, she blurted out the

Rusty Anchors

words anyway, anticipating a heated discussion: no, Arlaine didn't know anybody in the navy (yet), and yes, she did plan to attend.

Tildy was a wise and strict mother of five living, grown children. She would not even consider granting permission for her "beautiful daughter traipsing off, spending the evening with a shipload of hungry, gawking sailors who probably didn't even know how to dance." However, she'd seen that jitterbug nonsense, a far cry from respectable square dances at the church.

Never at a loss for words or the cleverness to dodge parental concerns, Arlaine concocted a rosier scenario: she wouldn't traipse off alone. Her two stunning sisters, Madelaine and Elaine, would attend the party with her—chaperones, if you will. Little did it matter if they had other plans! Arlaine had a way of cajoling even the most reticent of strong-willed sisters. Who knew how many tantrums it would take? But, as luck would have it, she convinced her sisters they would have a great time—and wore down her mother's reticence. Tildy assumed Madelaine, the senior sister, would yawn through the evening, bored but on duty. She already had a serious boyfriend whom the family, unfortunately, disliked. He was too old and worldly for Madelaine, they said. Perhaps, Tildy reasoned, a distraction aboard a ship might scuttle the ill-advised relationship. Any one of Tildy's daughters turned heads, and collectively, they were a bevy of beauties only the blind missed.

And so it was Tildy who reneged on the dance issue "just this once"—made a decision that changed lives forever. From that innocent encounter, Tildy was gifted (more than anyone could ever have imagined) with a future son-in-law, a slow boat to China, and a long and interesting posterity.

Shortly after the whirlwind courtship, Madelaine announced she was relocating to California to marry her beloved sailor. He was transferred to Treasure Island in the San Francisco Bay Area. She should have read the basic instruction manual before committing to becoming a navy wife. But instead, she quickly adapted to the changes and acknowledged that military life would never be easy. Unless dry-docked, sailors and ships seldom remain in port.

Doing their best to ignore all but each other, the newlyweds were deliriously happy. They rented a small apartment in the city and set up housekeeping. Assets consisted of plenty of nothing but mountains of joy, love, and dreams.

Of all coincidences, Ruth, Harold's absentee mother, unexpectedly became his borrow-a-cup-of-sugar neighbor. What were the odds of her moving from the South into the same apartment complex as her son? When the shock subsided, Ruth and her third husband, Jay, vowed they'd care for Madelaine when Harold was deployed. It wasn't unheard of, but it seemed odd that a strong bond of affection developed between the two most important women in Harold's life. Jay was an entirely different matter.

Scuttlebutt proved to be accurate, and within a matter of months, Harold explained he was being deployed—to China! The news was shocking. "Honey," he said, "we're gonna have to put our honeymoon on hold. I want you to join me as soon as you can."

Weeks later, Hal boarded the USS *Chaumont* and disappeared under the Golden Gate Bridge into a bank of a fog of ambiguity. Madelaine searched for a well-paying job. She rummaged through the *Chronicle*, looking for work, a way to pay for a ticket on a steamer heading eastward. Fortunately, Madelaine soon found a job at an exclusive country club, but living expenses were more than she wanted to pay. So, she returned to her family's home in Portland and found employment in more familiar surroundings. She couldn't afford to be moody, but the separation from the love of her life was unbearable.

Her sisters quizzed her about being a new bride, living in a famous metropolitan city, and speculations for the future. They questioned her sanity for running off, leaving them so suddenly, and opting for a new life none of them could scarcely fathom. Seldom at a loss for words, Madelaine had a lot to say. Foremost were expressions of joy and sadness because she and he were seas apart.

The girls reminisced about the chance meeting. Arlaine introduced the couple and promptly made snake eyes at several other pretty girls eyeing Harold. The ship boasted of good-looking, well-dressed young women. Perhaps it had been the handsome uniform that initially caught Madelaine's eye. Was it her silky yellow hair blowing in the wind or attractive curves he favored? Did it matter?

Hal was personable and a great dancer. He jitterbugged with the best of them, including Arlaine. But it was Madelaine that caused his jaw to drop. Arlaine, with complete seriousness, told gawking predators to get lost or she'd push them overboard! Nobody would hear the splash or miss them as they *accidentally* floated out to sea. It didn't take long for word to spread that nobody in their right mind messed with Arlaine!

Since that first serious discussion long ago over an apple in a garden named Eden, it would appear love was, and is, the glue that binds this crazy world together. In the summer of 1938, it was especially mystical for those watching and wondering. An eternal companionship suddenly developed between a couple of strangers on a ship within the banks of the deepest, widest river in the Northwest. Was it to be a metaphor for life's expectancies? She wondered.

History changed everything for a couple of strangers when the justice of the peace declared Miss Madelaine Lenoir Houghton to be Mrs. Harold William Foltz—and Arlaine took the credit. On that enchanted evening, a single line in Madelaine's journal said it all: "instantly falling in love was, for both of us, a powerful, forever experience; as if we'd known each other forever."

CHAPTER 21

House of Madelaine

"Come in," she said, "and play a while with me.
I am the little child you used to be."
—Henry Van Dyke

Harold said life was what it was, but it never made much sense. Aside from the navy, he knew for sure Madelaine was his world, his everything. She held him tightly and kissed his wetted cheeks. He seldom talked about life before they met, about his mother and the divorce.

"There will be no divorce in this household," Madelaine sternly affirmed. "Never!"

The couple vowed to work through the hard times that would surely come. And they swore the big D word (divorce) was never to pass between them. Never, never would they be divided. As though adding a new clause to the contract entered into at the altar, they mutually agreed to work extraordinarily hard to create a happy, loving home life for themselves and their posterity.

Cuddling intimately, Harold whispered, "Tell me about you."

"Where would you like me to start?" Madelaine inquired.

"At the beginnin'," he replied.

"I was born in the Rocky Mountains of Utah," she proceeded, "in a community of Swedish immigrants …"

On three frigid January days, five years apart, Ed and Tildy Houghton brought beautiful daughters into the world. Tildy called them her birthday surprises, as she too celebrated a January birthday. She smiled, envisioning future gaiety with her trio of angels. Like other families in rural areas, Tildy and Ed were eager to raise proper kinfolk.

The pretty, young mother dressed their youngsters in white bloomers, long white stockings, and hand-made cotton dresses. She tied satin ribbons on golden ringlets and blissfully kissed the chubby cheeks of her brood. With fairylike antics, the precious ones were reasons enough for life to overflow with joy.

Little Dorothy was the first of eight children. Immediately, she was the center of her parents' world, a precious child of promise. But, tragically, the infant lived only four unhealthy months. Tildy grieved and blamed herself for the untimely death. If only she'd listened to her heart instead of the cackling of do-well neighbors. Though it was commonplace to comingle healthy children with sickly ones, it never felt right to expose baby Dorothy to the cranky child with measles, but Tildy did it anyway. Hope was the well child would get it and recover quickly. "We do it all the time," crowed the wary neighbors.

Dorothy's parents meant well when they took their happy infant to the home of the ailing child. But another wreathing, miserable baby's cough was godawful.

Tildy's eyes widened as the toddler wailed, red with fever and sweat. Horrified, the young mother realized she'd made a terrible mistake. But the neighbors assured her the unhealthy child had a simple case of measles. Who knew the sick one had also been exposed to whooping cough and would soon die? Of course, baby Dorothy quickly acquired both diseases and was too ill to survive despite round-the-clock nursing and prayers.

Losing her baby was bitterer than the icy winds that sucked her life away. Heartbroken, the young mother dressed her lifeless baby in a christening gown and covered her with a small, hand-tied quilt. Tildy encased her ignorance in endless torment and emotional self-flagellation. With garlands of wildflowers and sympathetic tears, the tiny infant was interred among pioneer forbearers. Tildy forever blamed herself for listening, believing old wives' tales, and her pitiable misjudgment.

After the well-attended service, she gathered a few small, precious mementos and tenderly placed them in an old suitcase. She closed the lid, draped herself across it, and wept inconsolably. "There'll be others," the comforters whispered.

Two grief-stricken years passed before Tildy conceived again. In January, the second newborn was christened Vivian Leone. She was the image of her beautiful baby sister. Tildy said the infant was an answer to teary pleadings.

"There will be no visitors," she informed the community. "When I'm ready, I'll bring the baby to church for you to view, but she is not to be touched by anyone!" She insisted on advanced notices of any childhood illnesses, even as much as a runny nose. "And," she continued, "*no* children are to be brought to our home."

Three years later, Madelaine was born. Blond, blue-eyed, with Nordic clarity, she strongly resembled Dorothy and Vivian. The little ones were so easy to love. Charm could have been their middle name. Sparkling eyes and laughing voices epitomized their innocence and appeal. For Ed and Tildy, life in their turn-of-the-century home revolved around family—children. They were everything Tildy wanted.

Eddie's nickname for each of his little girls was "Daughter." Vivian giggled and simply called him "My Daddy!" If ever a child could mend wounded hearts muddling through insufferable losses, it was little Vivian. But as beautiful and tender as the children were, no one replaced the first. Doubly adored and doubly cherished, the births of Vivian and Madelaine were Tildy's hope for self-forgiveness. She loathed her previous ignorance and demonstrated her newly found competency with strictness, caution, and very close supervision.

Of English, French, and Indian ancestry, Eddy never considered his diminutive stature a hindrance to anything he put his mind to do. He was the son of pioneers who traveled west to settle in the mountains of Utah. Among his more exceptional attributes were his ethics of honesty and integrity. He was a God-fearing man, humble and hardworking, a true-blue family man. He worked various jobs—a skilled carpenter, miner, mechanic, laborer, and creative inventor. He gave his all to whatever the job required. Though not academically trained (few were in his time), Eddie was bright, highly motivated, and a quick learner. He knew work was always available in the mines. But Tildy worried about the dangers. Accidents were common—most often fatal. When jobs disappeared, mumblings among miners and other laborers alleged plenty of work in the Northwest. Hearsay whispered there was money to be made in lumber.

Madelaine was a newborn when Vivian, her precocious four-year-old sister, and their parents moved to the coast of Oregon. Eddie quickly found employment in a nearby lumber mill on the banks of the mighty Columbia. It seemed that luck was smiling when the family qualified for a cozy, company-owned cabin across the river from the mill. Far different from their homeland's mountains, the family found the treacherous sea, tall pines, and profitable deep, clear river new and exciting.

Each morning, the company whistle blew precisely at 7:00 a.m. Eddie and his newfound friends crossed over the swift, dangerous river. The sturdy bridge separated Eddie's work life from the responsibilities of home. He didn't mind the long, tedious hours and dismissed the dangers of learning new mill skills.

When the evening whistle blew, his family waited for him with delicious meals and plenty of love for dessert. Tildy baked tasty bread and was the best pie maker in the county!

Morning routines were as predictable as the swirling currents concealed by underbrush beside the old log homes. Awakening early, Eddie teased his giggling offspring while Tildy prepared a hearty breakfast. The morning whistle blew, and Eddie grabbed his tools and headed for the mill. With Vivian still clinging to his neck, Eddie tweaked the cheeks of the baby in her crib and, to her consternation, pinched his proper wife on the rump! He called her "Chub" and loved to hear her predictable chastisement, "Eddie!"

After the last nose-rub-kiss, Vivian pouted. "Oh, Daddy, I can hardly wait to see you at lunchtime. Watch for me. I'll be the one in a pretty white dress, crossing the bridge, carrying your lunchbox. Don't be sad to leave me," she glowered. "When I hear the whistle blow again, we can have another picnic by the river."

As promised, at noontime, the doll-like child scooped up Eddie's lunchbox and scurried across the bridge to meet him. From the kitchen window, her anxious mother observed as the golden-haired beauty sang and carefully skipped to her father. Then rushing to the front porch, she hollered, "Walk!" When Eddie's friendly hand wave signaled all was well, Tildy returned to the baby in the crib and other wifely chores.

Vivian, animated and cheerful, chattered as she and her doting father enjoyed Tildy's thick, chewy bread and sourdough cookies.

On Tildy's side of the river, she hummed, fastidiously tidying her home and caring for the baby. She was confident Vivian was safely in the hands of her gentle father. Picnic lunches with him were a daily practice unless the weather was incumbent. Two short toots of the whistle indicated lunchtime was over. Eddie folded a clean flour sack towel, placed it in the empty lunchbox, and handed it to the toddler. He thanked her profusely for keeping him company and made her promise to bring him another meal the following day—weather permitting.

"Oh, Daddy," she replied, "you know I always wait for you every day!" She hugged him tightly, enough to melt a wooden heart.

As workers moved toward the mill, Eddie walked her to the bridge and waved goodbye, repeating his warnings to be extra careful. Tildy also listened for the whistle, and when she heard it, she hurried to the front porch to greet Vivian as she skipped and sang noisily toward the safety of home. Once secure on her side of the river, the little one waved goodbye again to the small man with a loving heart. They laughed and blew wind-driven kisses into the air. Vivian was certain the cool breeze would carry them to her daddy's dimpled cheeks.

Eddie smiled and returned to his labors, confident he was the luckiest man ever born. When the piercing whistle wafted at eventide, tired workers shuffled to the bridge, where Vivian waited patiently. Though exhausted, Eddie tapped into some hidden source for energy to entertain his anxious imp, for the toddler was the music in his life. He read picture books and danced with her in his heavy boots—that is, until Tildy raised an eyebrow and pointed to her spick-and-span floor.

It was a typical gray afternoon on the coast, and Tildy was busy with the baby. She said she didn't hear the whistle. Sobbing hysterically, she'd taken her eyes off the child for only a moment, a moment that changed lives forever.

The notice in the newspaper read:

Little Vivian Houghton Drowned
The Four-Year-Old Tot Fell into the Millrace

> Vivian, the four-year-old daughter of Mr. and Mrs. E. W. Houghton, while playing along the bank of the millrace Tuesday afternoon, fell in and was drowned before help could rescue her. She was carried down the race for about 200 yards into the river, and down the river about the same distance, where her clothes caught on some bushes and lodged. She was in the water for at least one hour. Dr. Raymond was called and worked with the child for over an hour, but being in the water so long, the little one was chilled to death before she was taken out of the cold water. The alarm was given by the small son of Cal Larson, with whom the child had been playing. A number of neighbors joined in the search. When the body was recovered, the news of the death quickly spread and was responded to by a wave of sympathy from everyone in the community. The funeral was held at the LDS Church Wednesday afternoon at three o'clock.

A frenzied coworker said he saw two small children on the bridge arguing over a toy. It was Vivian's, hand-carved by her father. The little boy refused to give it back. A tug-of-war ensued. When the emergency alarm sounded, not even the husky lumberjacks could have saved the child. The doctor arrived almost immediately and said it was too late. Feverishly, Tildy pleaded with him to make her child live! Panic-stricken and hysterical, she insisted the child had been in the icy water for no more than twenty minutes. There might yet be a breath of life in the cold, wet little girl! The grieving mother was desperately beating on the doctor's chest, begging him to resuscitate her. But he refused, saying he was sure she was already gone.

When the lifeless, white-clad body was carried away, the shock of it sent Tildy into a deep, silent depression. Unmoved, she held the wet satin ribbons, staring at nothing at all—and nothing returned the gaze. No amount of sympathy or compassion fazed her. Why had death not called her instead? It was frightening to look into Tildy's tearless blue eyes and expressionless face. The few words in the obituary hardly tapped the events of that life-altering event.

Throughout the funeral service, Tildy sat motionless, tearless, deeply in shock. There was nothing more to be done for the little girl and nothing the mother could do for herself. Friends and family gathered as strangers tried to fill the needs of Tildy's family. But the young mother was too wounded to notice. Numbed by unfathomable grief, she went directly to her room and quietly closed the door. Alone, she curled into a fetal position on her soft, empty bed. She was confident; under the stately old pines, part of her own soul was buried that afternoon with her precious child in the freshly opened grave. The sight might have offered some sort of closure at the end of the day, but with time, the gravesite would become an all too familiar place.

It was springtime again, almost to the day she'd placed little Dorothy in her tiny grave, five years earlier. The wounds were still fresh and, with the new ones, hung together like bouquets of limp flowers, once vibrant and alive. Visions of her children resting peacefully in the arms of Mother Earth were simply too great for Tildy's fragile mind. They were hers, two lost children. It would have been easier to have died with them than to live without them.

Family and friends attempted to minister to Tildy's needs, but no amount of tender reasoning produced even a mustard seed of hope. The tragic losses were too profound, and the glaring facts would never change. All of her beloved children were gone, except Madelaine, crying softly in the next room.

Tildy stared unblinkingly, refusing to acknowledge any emotion at all. It was going to take a miracle for her to recover. Many well-wishers thought she had already drowned in the quicksand of her mind. Compassionately, they whispered she might never be well again.

"Not without my babies."

Tildy pulled the shades of hopelessness over her eyes and silently secreted herself to the farthest depths of emptiness—a warm, dark, comfortable place where no guests were invited. Perhaps she would never leave.

Church members, neighbors, and relatives rolled up their sleeves and walked the joyless hall, caring for the baby as they prayed for her mother. With little time for self-pity, Eddie carried his unfair burden of guilt and responsibility. If his precious child had not crossed the bridge that day—if only he'd waited a little longer to return to work—if only he'd not carved the little toy for her. Eddie wondered if somehow he'd offended Deity. He pondered the loss of two small daughters—and now a wife! Wringing his hands, he thought of the infant who needed her mother and a wife incapable of responding. He was wading in a sea of anguish, wondering how to cope. Though his heart was breaking, he hardly had time to mourn. If understanding were to come at all, it would have to wait. He was too busy juggling reality with necessity. And so it was with Madelaine's brokenhearted family.

Eddie and the doctor felt Tildy's instability might lessen if she could visit her extended family. Still, it was four long years before she recovered sufficiently to make the grueling trip. Traveling was arduous, especially with another toddler. She carefully folded Madelaine's white bloomers and cotton dresses and gazed longingly at her only living child. She was just the age of little Vivian when …

Eddie was full of trepidation as he kissed the two of them goodbye. He assured the cheerful toddler her trip by rail through the winding mountains would be exciting. "I'll miss you, Daddy. Can you come with us?"

"No, Daughter. I have work to do—and I'll miss you too. Send me a colored picture, and be a very good girl."

"I'll send you kisses on the wind and hugs through the clouds, Daddy."

Quietly among themselves, the Utah relatives pondered Tildy's impending visit. Her mental instability worried them, and they were confident the third little one would be spoiled and unmanageable. After all, she was their only surviving child. They felt sure the doting parents had produced a pampered little princess.

To their amazement, Madelaine danced and sang her way into their hearts. Sweet and obedient, intelligent and witty, she was respectful and amusing. Her cuteness and lovability helped mend Tildy's permanently saddened heart. She couldn't help smiling as the little child recited rhymes, poetry, and a litany of made-up stories. Later, she would win contests in school with her writing. They compared her to Longfellow! She recited humorous tales of huckleberries and bears in the thick green forests and other creatures that nibbled on the plants for fun.

In the years that followed, Tildy and Eddie gave birth to five more exceptional and well-loved children.

In her declining years, Tildy kept an old suitcase secreted in the back of a closet. She opened it only occasionally and touched the contents with reverence. More than one grandchild asked, "Whose old toys are those, Grandma? Tell us about the little white dresses, the baby shoes, and the pretty white ribbons. May we play with the little boy toys?"

Tildy firmly replied, "They're my special things, and no, you may not even touch them! Promise me you will never open my suitcase or get into my things, ever." She didn't ask much in life, but these small items were hers, sacred and private. Carefully, she repacked the aging treasures and latched the old case. White-haired and aging before her time, the distant look in her eyes bespoke of hidden reminiscences, of little children, running, laughing, and picking wildflowers in the springtime.

What balm is it that soothes the soul? Time, they say—only time.

Madelaine (on right) with her Russian friend, Nina, on the ship Tatau Maru en route to China (1940)

Nancy at Nana's (1943)

On Left:
The Foltz Family (Harold and Madelaine, David and Nancy, 1943)

On right:
Harold as chief, US Navy

CHAPTER 22

The Buddy They Loved

Oregon, 1924

And three made four. The newborn was a son whom Harold and Madelaine joyously named David—David Harold. Bright-eyed and handsome, he was a happy baby and clearly the apple of his mother's eye. Harold grinned, holding the infant in his arms. At last, he was not only a father; he had a son!

David resembled Madelaine's little brother, Ronald, who unfortunately drowned when he was only six. Blue-eyed and blond, the family called him Buddy. They chuckled as he grew, watching the little guy follow Madelaine like a duckling on the prowl. His big sister was in her early twenties and often entertained him while Tildy cared for her large family, including six children, two sets of aging in-laws, and a few other miscellaneous relatives! Born premature, Tildy determined her little Buddy was going to live a happy, healthy life—never dreaming that before he reached the age of accountability, she'd place him in a grave next to little Vivian.

One lazy afternoon, Buddy begged his older brother, Lavon, to take him to the beach for a picnic. "Don't take your eyes off him," Tildy warned. But adolescence, being what it was, drew Lavon's attention to unexpected friends, laughing and playing, already frolicking in the water. Lavon said it was only a minute or two—and the little guy was gone. They discovered him facedown in the millrace a half mile downstream. The family, all too familiar with drownings and death, grieved deeply, especially Madelaine, who thought of him as her own.

Lavon, of course, was shattered. The loss opened new and unhealable wounds. He placed sole responsibility for the tragedy upon his own shoulders. Somewhere deep in his soul, he hung grief and shame on the walls of his psyche—wounds from which he remained guilt ridden for the remainder of his life. He refused to be comforted or accept the soothing balm of forgiveness. He couldn't understand how his beloved mother could continue to love him despite the accident; that he was forgiven of his folly or, as her only living son, they could grieve together, bury the past, and move forward. Try as she did, Tildy couldn't hide her sorrow. Buddy's death only deepened the grief for having already buried three of her precious children. Madelaine and her family attended services in the pouring rain, another test of Tildy's faith and courage. Time, she hoped, would soften the pain—but it never did.

Madelaine rocked her own little son and told God she would protect him from everything that could possibly harm him. He was a blessing she would cherish throughout eternity. One husband, one daughter, one son—that's all she ever wanted.

CHAPTER 23

Voices in the Fog

West Oakland, California, 1944

Shadowy, thick fog often rolled across the bay. It was possible, with keen alertness, to feel the hushed, rolling spectacle before it arrived. It enveloped the city and its inhabitants with a chilling, impenetrable blanket of near blindness.

The silence was eerie. Ships, trees, tall buildings, even the bay itself seemed to disappear in the misty silence. It was as if cackling witches were camouflaging impending misdeeds. The night sky, usually clear and darker than blueberries, disappeared, and it seemed even mornings delayed their arrivals.

On lonely nights, a powerful, low-toned horn rumbled endless intermittent warnings. Its throbbing vibrations filled the air with uneasiness. Prudence slowed to a crawl and bid the wise to follow suit. Neighborhood drunkards staggered uncaringly and snickered as they belched in close rhythm with the horn.

The growling foghorns made it challenging to sleep. The low, melancholy, cautionary rumble caused the air to vibrate; their warnings gave sailors and anglers a sense of guarded security but frightened little children and caused wet cats to howl in the dark.

Often, our mamma bear invited her anxious children into her room and invented distracting bedtime stories. The chatter fueled imaginations with slow-moving ships, luxury liners, and fishing vessels crawling blindly through the chilly seas. Wise mariners always trusted the voice of the powerful, unseen horn and progressed stealthily through the sightless sheets.

Madelaine was alone and vulnerable with two small children, and she knew it.

"Honey, you'll be glad to know that Lavon is moving to California," she wrote. "He's a gifted welder and has absolutely no fear of heights! He'll be working on the Golden Gate Bridge."

Her brother was a looker, so the ladies said. Conveniently, he rented an apartment directly across the street from his sister and was helpful with everything Madelaine needed. He impishly brought candy treats for a couple of navy kids waiting for normalcy to dock on special occasions. Lavon was well liked and never at a loss for company—especially the female kind. His personality was intense, often reckless, a man who lived and worked on the outer edges of caution. If he'd used a spiritual net, it might have saved him from a string of broken hearts and unwise choices, but he didn't. He chose to live by his own set of rules and tossed caution to the wind—thinking perhaps the safety harness he often wore in his profession was enough to protect him from the tragedies of life.

On one of those foggy nights, Lavon introduced his sister to a voluptuous redhead who gave birth to his two young sons, David and Gary. They were just our ages. "Cousins and playmates are a good combo." He grinned, and indeed they were.

Madelaine finally felt a measure of safety, knowing that help had moved just across the street—mostly when strange, unfamiliar sounds filled the cold, wet air.

"Snuggle down in the covers," she said, 'because Oregonians always sleep with open windows and breathe the cool night air."

"What's an Oregon-un?" I asked.

"Never mind." She yawned. "I'll tell ya some other time."

Changing from reality to fairy tales, she continued. "The damp air is cleansing the earth. In the morning, we'll find sidewalks and flowers washed by Mother Nature's Fog Service." She said not even the moon shined on foggy nights, and birds snuggled more in depth into their

Rusty Anchors

nests. Of course, she was believed, though the unwholesome sounds continued to permeate the gloominess.

Mamma talked for a long time—that is, I spoke. She yawned and stretched, waiting for me to run out of words. When she stopped moving and I was sure she was asleep, I chattered gently to the baby nestled at the foot of her bed. Little David was a planned present from her sweetheart's last visit.

I spoke ever so softly, bending over an improvised bassinette, a large basket lined with cozy blankets. Even then, the baby wasn't much fun. He hardly moved. Blinking sleepily, he drank his milk and dozed. If only the world embraced the joy and peace of the moment, Mamma said, but he was too busy slumbering to pay attention to her or his nearly three-year-old sister. So I tucked the blankets around his neck and scampered quietly back to the warmth and security of Mamma's bed.

It was on one of those early foggy mornings that we heard rapping at the front door. Hurrying down the steep wooden stairs, Mamma moved the curtain aside and peered gingerly into the fog. Dressed in nightclothes, I followed.

A tall visitor holding a heavy duffel bag stood patiently on the steps. It was Daddy—the elusive sailor in the picture beside Mamma's bed. His brief, infrequent, and unexpected visits were usually unannounced. It was easy to forget who he was and what he was all about. Only the dark blue uniform was consistent. Mamma squealed and swung open the door. "You're home!" she exclaimed.

The stranger focused his complete attention upon her as we pitter-pattered up the narrow stairway. In her room, he picked up the basket and peered at the wide-eyed infant, his only son. Then turning to Mamma, he grinned and said, "Where'd ya get this little guy?"

The man put his hands on his slender hips, like me, and tilted his head. He always asked the same questions: "Are you Nancy? You're all growed-up. Let's measure you against the other pencil marks on the wall and see how much you've grown since I was last here."

Though the city was fogged in, the circle of love in the tiny apartment was evident. By midmorning, the sun peeked shyly through the haze. True to her word, the *service* was still busy washing sidewalks and watering lawns.

Mamma was right—she was always right. The foghorn beckoned vessels away from harm as they passed under the Golden Gate. And the angry world seemed a little brighter, cleaner—and happier. The foghorn warning blessed seafarers waiting for wives and small children. Indeed, life was serene simply because—for the present—Daddy was home.

CHAPTER 24

Agnes of Oakland

Oakland, California, 1946

It was another foggy morning by the bay, and Mamma was going to tell me to run along and play, but she was busy with her little son and forgot. So, I dressed in yesterday's play clothes and a warm sweater. Helping myself to a stool, I unlatched the front door, closed it quietly, and skipped down the sidewalk, hoping to find a playmate or two.

As if by happenstance, I crossed the quiet street. Skipping by a set of small apartments across the lawn from cousins David and Gary, to my surprise, there she stood: a new child on the block with porcelainlike hands holding tightly to the knob of the freshly painted door. It seemed as though she might have been concerned about the wind blowing her away, but there was no wind—just calm gray fog.

The child was the most beautiful little girl I'd ever seen—exquisite in every detail. Startled at the unexpected discovery, especially one as stunning as she, I stopped to ask her name.

"Agnes," she responded.

"Agnes?" I asked.

"Yes," she replied, "and this is our new house."

She didn't look like any of the other neighborhood children. They played in the sandbox or roller-skated down the walkway and were usually quite dirty, but not Agnes.

No, Agnes was different, more doll-like than real dollies that sat obediently on the shelves at Macy's. I'd never seen any child that looked like Agnes. She could have been a real-live storybook princess if only she'd worn a tiara. She had the face of an angel; her pink lips turned upward in the corners. Her large blue eyes were bright and inquisitive. Beautiful golden ringlets hugged her shoulders, and satin ribbons matched her frilly dress.

Very occasionally, Agnes appeared outside with her mother. They ambled gracefully down the sidewalk. Everything about the child was brand-new—including Agnes herself! Even her patent leather shoes and long white stockings were spotless and fresh.

Unlike our other playmates, Agnes never romped in the grass, roller-skated, or participated in any of our games. Amusing myself, I imagined her on my team playing Kick the Can. She probably didn't even have a can, and if she did, no one ever kicked it—not even Agnes. Her mother was lovely too, but she never visited any of the neighbors. Agnes followed her example to a tee.

One breezy afternoon as the fog was lifting, Mamma announced we were going across the street to visit with family. She grabbed a plate of freshly baked peanut butter cookies and wrestled with her key.

"Put on your coat; it's time to go," she said.

Little David and I bundled up warmly and followed her like a couple of goslings heading for a pond. When we neared her residence, I mumbled, "That's where Agnes lives."

"Who's Agnes?" Mamma asked. I was just about to tell her when our happy cousins greeted us at their doorway. Our mothers, as usual, began chattering nonstop. Mamma passed the plate to our thoughtful aunt as her youngest son, Gary, stood in the corner of the room, sucking his thumb.

"You kids take some treats and go outside to eat 'em," Mamma said.

Cousins were always our best playmates. We dug roads in the sandbox and added hills and dales for realism. But when Mamma said, "I have things to do at home. Let's go, kids!" playtime was over. We gathered our toys and said our goodbyes until the next playtime.

Unexpectedly, Agnes and her mother suddenly left their apartment as we were saying our final farewells. Though not alone, I was among the most apparent gawkers. We watched them gliding along the public sidewalk, queenlier than anyone could imagine. It appeared to be an oversight that someone didn't roll out the red carpet, but the heads-up pair hardly acknowledged the omission. Trikers stopped riding, dirt throwers froze, and women hanging wet clothes on heavily ladened clotheslines stood at attention until Agnes and her mother passed. Unfazed and stoic, the pair promenaded before our very eyes! They hardly blinked as neighbors and vendors stepped aside, watching but not daring to speak even to one another until the neighborhood royals were out of sight.

Agnes pushed a lifelike baby doll in what appeared to be a brand-new carriage. I'd never seen such treasures and was sure that she had more new toys than anyone else hidden behind her door. I wondered about them.

Clip-clop. Clip-clop. Agnes moved gracefully, pushing a bright pink doll carriage. One small, gloved hand was pressed securely into her mother's. I was surprised when, without breaking her measured stride, Agnes suddenly turned and smiled. My chin dropped as I watched her disappear down the long gray sidewalk.

I turned to the cousins—grimy from a hard morning of kid play.

"Why doesn't she ever come outside and play with us?" I asked.

Cousin David pointed toward her door, noting that she lived only a stone's throw from his apartment.

"She never leaves her apartment and never plays outside," he said, "and she doesn't have any brothers or sisters." It seems Agnes was an only child.

Between all of us, the four cousins, we knew everyone under four feet tall—except her. No one was certain how long she'd lived there, and Gary said nobody knew her name. I was about to tell him, but David said he knew her.

"OK," I replied, "then who is she?"

Calmly, he replied, "Agnes of Oakland!"

"Where's her daddy?" I asked.

"I dunno," the cousins replied. "Maybe he's away at war, like yours."

"Well, why doesn't she ever come outside and play?"

Disinterested, cousin David shrugged his shoulders and dropped to his knees in a new patch of dirt. He was busy making roads with his scuffed-up, orange-colored tractor. He handed me a little yellow car. "Here," he said. "You can drive on my roads. I just made 'em."

He was much kinder and shared his treasures much better than I did. The barren spot of land in the middle of his patchy lawn was ideal for bulldozing make-believe roadways and for watching Agnes's apartment. The cousins said she was different. As if they read my mind, Gary continued, "And nobody plays inside her apartment either!"

The more Agnes didn't play with us, the more we wanted to play with her. We (outside kids) romped in the sunshine noisily, tattered and contented. Daring one another, occasionally one of our friends rang her doorbell and asked, "Can Agnes come out and play?"

The answer was always the same: "Agnes doesn't play outside." Her mother didn't give us time to ask why not. We knew she played with her dollies inside her house, but we had no idea why she never was dirty, didn't jump rope, and was an entirely different kind of child. We were confident she didn't even know about the sandbox, the swings, or slides behind the apartments.

Occasionally, we played extra noisily near her front door, hoping to attract her attention. But it appeared she didn't hear or see the other waiflike children or us at all—though very sporadically, having aroused her curiosity, she pushed the drapes aside and surveyed a flock of grimy, grinning imps.

One day, I was surprised to note Agnes was watching me from her sequestered solitude. I smiled and waved. Her eyes blinked, and she appeared surprised. Unexpectedly, she grinned sweetly and peered at me as though she wanted to wave back. But she didn't. And, as usual, her mother gently removed her from the window and closed the drapes.

Waiting for her return was useless. She didn't come back. I wondered what she might be doing in that quiet, lonely place, but I never knew for sure. No one did. Heavy drapes were usually drawn tightly across her mysterious apartment windows. Except for the empty milk bottles on her porch, the place looked deserted. Occasionally, the drapes hung limply, slightly parted, and we spotted Agnes watching us play.

The spotless windows made her seem closer as she sat in silence on the other side of the wall. We could almost touch her. But if she stood at the window for more than a few minutes, her mother, who never seemed to see us at all, slowly picked up the child and closed the curtains, and the two of them disappeared from view. Her ever-unhurried mother did not display any emotion. Behind the drapes, the two of them lived quietly, surrounded by ambiguity. Only occasionally did the enigmatic woman and her doll-like child leave their quarters. And, from the manner of their attire, we were confident they were going someplace special.

Agnes was different from every stranger I've ever known, not at all like my cousins or any of the children with whom we played and grappled. She was a princess child, a puzzling little girl who, if she'd ever really known me, might have been my best friend. But since she never did, she is only recalled as a tiny child sitting alone behind panes of glass, friendless, protected, and obedient.

"Who did you say she was?" Mamma asked.

Still holding her pretty mamma-sized hand, I looked at her and smiled.

"Agnes," I replied. "She was almost my best friend—almost."

CHAPTER 25

Need a Lift?

You cannot direct the wind—but we can adjust the sails.
—Bertha Calloway

California roads were narrow and underdeveloped in the 1940s. The talk was, one day, a grand highway would stretch the entire length of the state. Skeptics scoffed at such an idea as tractors, farm equipment, machinery of all sorts, buses, and autos traveled the monotonous two-lane roads together. Hundreds of miles of the country's most fertile agricultural farmlands filled the San Joaquin Valley.

North-to-south and south-to-north trips were tedious—sometimes dangerous. It wasn't a ride for people with a low tolerance for boredom. The valley's views were uncomfortably dull unless one had a keen interest in onion fields, tomatoes, garlic, grapevines, strawberries, oranges, and numberless crops mile after everlasting mile. When we passed the grapefruit and walnut groves, it was time to get out and stretch.

However, the coastal, more scenic route was slower, curvy, most often foggy, and treacherous, especially at night. Though she preferred traveling near the sea, depending upon the time of year and the weather conditions, Mamma usually traversed the dusty inland route. She alleged the state had only two seasons, hot and golden, green and cold. We traveled both—complaining all the way.

Winter driving was all the more dangerous. Low-lying tule fog covered the valley floor as Mamma strained to see through the thick murkiness. Droning automobiles crawled in ghostly fashion, hoping the road ahead was straight and unencumbered. The alternate route along the coastline was worse. Vehicles were forbidden to use headlights as a matter of national security; any light might aid enemies planning land assaults. Blackouts were mandatory. Daring drivers moved cautiously, but occasionally, misfortunes made headlines. Jagged cliffs and sudden curves claimed more than one tense daredevil.

Mamma was not a naïve navigator. She was a petite, map-memorizing soul who perhaps never should have been underestimated by strangers needing a lift.

An unusual incident began when Mamma received an exciting letter from the chief. He said he was docking in Long Beach for a few days. Could we possibly join him? When his ship pulled into any port on the West Coast, Mamma always hurried to the man she loved. She plotted the shortest, fastest trip, usually southward. Experience taught her when and how to journey with children, especially in the hot summer months. Before the crack of dawn, she refilled the desert water bag and unceremoniously piled two sleepy kids onto the back seat of the car, pajamas, pillows, and all. A nearby cardboard box held readily available necessities. She grabbed her bags, locked the door, and sped into the promise of dawn.

To the first kid who stirred, she'd whisper, "It's not time to awaken. Sleep as long as you can." She meant that the longer we rested, the quieter, less cantankerous we were apt to become. Traveling on supreme faith in an old vehicle that struggled to pass inspection for making the long trip safely, she packed sandwiches, snacks, and miscellaneous entertainment for her kids.

"Smell that before you eat it," she said of unrefrigerated food on long, long trips.

When the speedometer reached fifty, she gripped the steering wheel all the tighter. With a couple of rambunctious bouncers in the back, her maps were strewn across the front seat (with no relief driver in sight). She prided herself on reaching the destination as quickly and safely as possible. Without taking her eyes off the road, she could swat a couple of sparring youngins or lull them to sleep with endless figments of her imagination. Talking kept her coherent, she said.

In the heat of the day, she rolled down the windows, shared a jug of lukewarm water, and occasionally passed a few jellybeans. "Suck the candy so it will last longer," she said. It never did. And once gone, watching the world whiz by one fertile field after another was mind-numbingly repetitious. David and I warred with tediousness and each other: "Are we almost there? Will we be stopping soon? How much longer? We have to go to the bathroom!" The latter was sure to get her attention. Where was an entirely different matter. "Soon," she said.

Verdant farmlands attracted millions of insects swarming in tight formations—and an occasional loner looking for a thrill. If the bugs weren't flying, they crawled, humming loudly and eyeing ways to annoy humans. It was dangerous maneuvering through veils of bugs, but Mamma did it anyway! Low-flying creepy-crawlies hovered in front of the windshield, daring her to hit them. Ruthless gamblers! Large, juicer pests challenged her to miss them. She seldom did.

It wasn't unusual for insects to invite themselves into the stuffy automobile. Steering, swearing, and swatting—Mamma wished she was the only motorist on the road, as did farmhands and other swerving drivers. Who knew she was a tired, determined navy wife traveling with annoying distractions and cantankerous kids? Her impatience grew all the more transparent as the hours dragged on. Maneuvering on dusty, pitted detours, crawling behind slow-moving machinery, juggling well-worn maps, and edgy kids grew all the more exhausting.

Someplace just after sundown and way past fatigue, she planned to stop for the night if she could find a clean, cheap motel. But lodgings were scarce, funds were short, and she often pushed herself "just another hour or two." Our fretfulness ranked far below her determination to plow through the valley and into the arms of her sweetheart. On she went, though sleep would have taken the sting from her eyes and refreshed her senses.

Finally, Mamma pulled into a nearly deserted gas station. She hoped to find the lowest price for a couple of gallons of fuel and the quickest service that returned her to the road. A stickler for safety, she ordered us to wait in the hot car and keep the doors locked as she fueled the tank. Impatiently, we expected to stretch our legs as she pumped gas. Doing her best, she tried to avoid flying and scurrying crickets. From the back seat, we fought over who would dip the scrub brush into the water bucket and rinse bug guts from the windshield neither of us could reach. When the car was ready, she climbed onto the running board and struggled with her short-armed window washing technique. Unfortunately, she smeared greasy splotches across the glass and muttered profanities under her breath. Scrubbing harder, she cursed the petrified remains. Her red-and-white checkered dress swung wildly in the summer heat.

Plunking down a dollar for fuel, she returned to the car and cheerlessly escorted me to the outhouse. It was easy to find: follow the flies! A well-worn trail of dried yellow weeds always led straight to the wooden seats. She opened the ghastly door and, side by side, we gagged on necessity.

"Keep your mouth covered," she mumbled. "The filthy flies are sociable!"

She ran to the locked car and handed little David a large coffee can that read "Good to the last drop."

"Aim well!" she ordered.

"Don't look!" My brother frowned. Of course, I did!

Pitifully whining, I said, "I hate those stinky potties and the slivers on those old seats. Why don't I ever get to use the coffee can?"

Mamma replied, "Don't complain. It's a plumbing issue."

Before continuing our arduous trip, David spotted a picture of an ice-cream cone in the gas station window. When she spotted a small sign inviting us to lick, Mamma handed the greasy mechanic the money and treated us to something cold.

"It should taste good," she said as the orange ooze moved slowly down our arms. "Lick faster!"

We met an old coot at that lonely filling station. Miles from anywhere, the unkempt stranger approached our parked car, begging for a lift to the next town.

Always cautious with strangers, it must have been the heat of the sun that moved her to pity the scraggly, pathetic old man. She asked what he was doing in the "Land of Desolation." She inquired where he was going and how he happened to be alone in the remote valley. He said someone dropped him off at the station, left him, and he'd been waiting for some kindly soul to give him a ride to the next town.

Feeling uneasy but sorry for the sweaty old geezer, she reluctantly agreed to drive him to the next Podunk village—somewhere down the road. Through miles and fields of boredom, he sat stoically next to Mamma. Before long, the stranger nodded off. His jaw bounced loosely, and periodically, he snorted himself awake. His breath would have made a swine grimace. As Mamma drove, the head of the tired old man bounced closer and closer toward her shoulder.

"What's that smell?" David asked.

Making eye contact with him through the rearview mirror, Mamma waved her finger in the air, shook her head no, and rolled down the window. We sat motionless for several more reeking miles. Mamma didn't want to believe it, but David whispered swarms of nasty black flies were following us!

Suddenly, a slow-moving tractor turned onto the road directly in front of us. Pallets of wooden crates obstructed the view until it was too late. Mamma swerved, hit the brakes hard, and barely missed the tractor resting in a cloud of dust. As a protective reaction—modus operandi for her—she flung her arm across the seat, protecting passengers from spiraling forward. But on this trip, we weren't in the seat next to her.

Before she could apologize or explain, Mr. Coot awakened, wondering why Mamma appeared to be groping his chest. He turned toward her, grinned amorously, and grabbed her hand and arm. The old guy mistook her motherly gesture as an invitation for romance. Snuggling uncomfortably close to the speeding driver, he continued to press her hand toward him, passionately working his way up her extended arm with uninvited kisses. Shocked, Mamma maneuvered the car with one hand and pushed at the old man with the other. Cursing, she swerved dangerously back and forth across the highway.

"What on earth are you doing?" she screeched.

"I didn't know you cared." The stranger beamed. Unbuttoning his dirty shirt, he reeked of time and days-old sweat. Afraid she'd have an even more significant, more serious confrontation if she stopped the car, she floored it. Purposely and dangerously, it swayed from one side of the road to the other.

The frightened stranger bellowed, "Slow down! You're a scarin' the hell outta me! Let me outta here, blondie! You're the worst-est driver I ever knowed. Slow down afore you gets us kilt!"

"Take your paws off me," Mamma demanded, "or I'll strangle you with my bare hands!"

The old car swayed like a hula dancer with diarrhea. Suddenly, it screeched to a halt, engulfing us in a cloud of dust. Indians for miles read the grimy message: crazy lunatic about to hit the pavement!

Leaning precariously across the lecherous, misguided stranger, Mamma did her best to avoid the dirty hands and arms that seemed to be everywhere at once. She opened his door and booted the surprised would-be Romeo onto the dusty roadside. Stunned, he scrambled away from the harebrained woman maneuvering the unsteady vehicle. David and I stared in wonderment. As we sped away, the old man was still reaching in midair for answers. He only wanted to kiss her!

It was hard to tell if Mamma was more upset with the careless tractor, the geezer's inappropriate behavior, or her misjudgment. But she stomped on the gas, and the car lurched forward in complete obedience. We watched the dusty stranger scramble to his feet—definitely alone in the middle of nowhere—and chase our speeding vehicle.

Mamma glanced in the rearview mirror only once. Holding onto the steering wheel with both hands, she was cussing a blue streak, annoyed with her irresponsible decision to help a sorry traveler—and the tractor that could have killed us. If she'd been in a better mood, she might have tossed the nasty old man a couple of aspirin. Indeed, confused and astounded, he most likely had a headache worth forgetting.

She was still shaking when I innocently asked, "Who was that man?" David was speechless.

"A problem," she muttered. "A huge mistake—with a rough ending!"

For the next hundred miles, she answered a barrage of kid questions. The scary experience made the typically monotonous trip unusually gripping. We had plenty to talk about when we met the chief in Long Beach. He asked Mamma to promise *never* to give a stranger a ride to anywhere, regardless of the circumstances. That was a promise she religiously kept.

Want a lift? Not even a crazy man would ask a pretty little navy wife with two troublesome kids in the back seat of an old car for that kind of adventure. Henceforth, it never bothered Mamma to leave numberless coots stuck in strange smelling places with only friendly flies for company.

Need a ride? ... Don't even think about it!

CHAPTER 26

Paddlin' Madelaine

Portland, Oregon, 1946

The neighborhood wasn't getting any safer, but the last straw broke as Harold was at sea on an extended cruise: a neighborhood child from Madelaine's complex was abducted sometime in the middle of the night.

The horror of it was traumatizing. Madelaine began religiously locking every window and double-checking her work through the long, foggy nights. Strange sounds kept her awake. Soon, every unexpected noise sent her tiptoeing in the dark, checking on the safety of her kids, ages three and five. She wrote to her sisters in Portland about her fright, and they too were duly alarmed.

"Madelaine, why don't you pack up a few things and come stay with us until Harold gets home again?"

With that generous invitation, she headed for safety—paddling into adventures never to be forgotten. Her daily letter writing continued, though Oregon's vast Willamette River often watermarked the envelopes.

The sister chatter resumed the moment Mamma's suitcases touched Elaine's front porch. Of course, she had room for us … "For a while," chimed in her husband, Elmer. It was his way of attempting to shade the truth with his humorless brand of hospitality.

The ever-close sisters were grateful to be together again. They knitted sentences together as though miles and months of separation were inconsequential. It wasn't necessary to say, "Now, where were we?" as old and new topics flowed freely in rapid succession.

Elaine was eager for Madelaine to see their new boat. Just the mention of a vessel lighted Elmer's world. He was a yachtsman's yachtsman and loved anything that floated; the bigger, the better. However, he wasn't fond of distractions—like Mamma and the kids. He very much favored the socially elite, people with titles, big boats, and caviar on crackers. Though, in certain circles, he feigned tolerance for broods of fellow yachters on smaller crafts. The day following Madelaine's arrival, the sisters added Arlaine to the crowd and headed to the yacht club, kids in tow.

En route, a group of tied-up houseboats caught Madelaine's attention. The race was on for information about a rental that she had noticed only for curiosity's sake. It sported a clearly visible sign: "For Sale. Telephone 7274."

The proprietor was eager to unload the aging craft and made Madelaine a deal she couldn't resist. Faster than patrolling speedboats, she whipped out a pen and signed on the dotted line. Wouldn't Petty Officer Foltz be surprised when her next letter arrived? She was sure he'd respond, "You bought a what on the where?" and, smiling, she wasn't disappointed when he did!

The houseboat was fully furnished, albeit with aging fittings and a few moldy throw rugs. The entire unit was at least twenty years overdue for attention. Madelaine saw past the challenges, bought cans of paint, scrubbed, sanded, and bellowed at her two curious kids (for safety's sake) in very close quarters.

When at last her nails were shot and she was dog-tired, the unit was finally family ready. She climbed on a stool, hung her favorite pink sheer curtains, and snuggled contentedly with two kids in her swaying bunk. Placing a treasured, framed picture of Harold covered with kid kisses next to the bunk, she declared the rocking craft to be home sweet home.

"There you go, honeybunch," she whispered. "We have a nautical home—our first!"

She promised we'd have more in common with her petty officer when we gained our sea legs and learned to live on the water as he did. At first, the steady rocking movement was terrifying, and we felt sick.

"You're developing little sea legs. You'll get used to them," Madelaine promised. "In a few days, you won't notice the movement. Remember, we're Scandinavians, kin of Vikings! Boat life is in our blood. Your Nordic ancestry should be kickin' in soon. For now, eat, breathe—and sleep in those life jackets! And don't remove them unless I say so!"

Swaying and gawking at a whole new world was fodder for many scribbled letters. Madelaine wrote about "shady characters" hanging around the area. They made her nervous, especially when she heard whisperings in the dark and hoped no one was on her slippery, freshly sanded deck. In silence, she glided through the darkened living quarters, moved aside the curtain for a better view, and prayed. She hoped that perhaps it was just the wind or the rain. In his letters, the petty officer reminded her to keep the hatches battened. By the time his next letter arrived, security was down to an artform—day and night.

Moored on a busy waterway, the deck attached to the houseboat was a perfect podium for squawking wildlife observing marine animals and boat traffic. Ducks perched on the railing, quacking for bread crumbs. Their playfulness and the boat's constant motion was an ever-present reminder of the river's incessant delights and hazards. Stringent rules forbade unsupervised or unjacketed kids on the deck. They knew the river was strong and uncaring, and one careless slip spelled disaster.

On sunny afternoons, the contented threesome watched rafts of logs towed to the paper mill downstream—and other ever-changing scenarios. Oh yes, the river bustled with activity. Wakes rocked the houseboat with authority. Sometimes deep-throated whistles blew from passing vessels, and workers waved. Perhaps it was Mamma in her shorts that caught their attention, but the children were confident the friendly horns were tooting just for them.

When Madelaine was finally sure the houseboat was ready for company, her sisters' names were at the top of the list.

Elmer drove Elaine to the river. Honking for attention, he parked his new car under a bank of trees. Sporting his best nautical wear, he waved and strutted like a peacock to the dock. Elaine clutched the hand of her little girl and followed. Madelaine smiled and waved enthusiastically. Her hair was tied up with a bandana that did nothing to hide the fresh smudges on her forearms. She mumbled something about the wet paint as she rushed to greet her cheerful family.

"This still wet?" Elmer asked. Perhaps it was the smell that alerted him to the fresh paint on the flimsy railing and planks leading to the boathouse.

"Come on in and see what we've been doing."

David and I were running down the dock unescorted, following Mamma. Uneven planks swayed, reminders of the dangers we chose to ignore. Swaying unsteadily, we hoped Mamma had forgotten the security policies that she had placed on us. She and Elaine plainly understood the hazards of mixing kids with river water. Still, it felt good to be on land again, and David and I temporarily ignored the stern warnings.

Elmer must have misinterpreted our enthusiasm.

Suddenly, everything holy broke loose. He grinned at Janice, grabbed me, and hoisted me to his chest. I was startled; he didn't like me, and we both knew it. A power rush obviously clouded his sanity, and with reckless abandonment, he leaned forward, suspending me headfirst over the freshly painted railing. I peered into the deep, murky river. Amusing himself, Elmer hooted at the power he temporarily displayed. He was a cold, spoiled man with complete control of a scared little girl.

"What's she worth to you?" he said.

Mamma's wordless mouth fell open, her face ashen. Even on a good day, she never liked him—and this suddenly was not a good day! But before she could speak, Elmer tossed me aside carelessly and scooped little David into his arms. Cackling, he swung the terrified, squirming toddler over the water, beyond the less-than-secure railing, by one leg. The poor little guy was gasping for air, hardly able to breathe. The child looked at Mamma, then at the water, and screamed. Mamma's eyes darted between the horrified child, merciless river, and foolhardy man.

An only child, Elmer always had an overinflated sense of self-worth. He was controlling and sported a cruel sense of superciliousness toward those he considered less than his equal. But he made a terrible mistake thinking Madelaine would acquiesce to his idiocy. Her eyes were red with fury as she lunged forward, pouncing on him like a panther. Clenching her teeth, she sank her fingernails into his flesh like a vice—a maniac demanding the immediate return of her little son. Elmer was stunned. She didn't appreciate his attempt at humor. He lowered the child obediently, at which point Mamma snatched her son and handed the petrified child to her speechless sister.

Elmer towered above his sister-in-law, but she—shaking with wrath—pressed him against the unstable railing for a *discussion*. It's a miracle the old boards stayed in place. Using every swear word in her extensive vocabulary with ear-piercing volume, she barred him from ever touching her children again—or boarding her home. Wide-eyed, the man was speechless but clearly understood every syllable sent through her clenched jaw—especially the cussing. Oh yes, he completely understood. She had no sense of humor, none at all!

The aquatic family affair was short-lived, fiery, and long remembered as the impetus for terminating her family's nautical lives. "For Sale" signs and arrows pointed the way to the freshly decorated site—and the houseboat changed ownership quickly. Profit from the sale was enough for train tickets back to Oakland, California.

Who needs that much excitement? Indeed, the uncertainties of war provided more than enough anxiety in ours. Perhaps Elmer's foolish, venomous behavior had starkly brought to the forefront, in Madelaine's mind, how her siblings' tragic losses could very well happen to one of her children. Thus, the three of us were dry-docked for life ever since—and mighty glad of it.

CHAPTER 27

"That's My Daddy!"

"All aboard!" hollered the conductor. Belching steam and chugging impatiently, the train was raring to go.

Mamma was out of breath. Eager not to be late, she dragged her kids along the covered platform to the rapidly filling compartments. Our little legs strained to keep up with her. One might have thought the baggage she carried would have slowed her down, but she compensated for the awkwardness with the skill of a gazelle.

"Move along!" she ordered.

Careful not to notice the little woman and two small children, the busy crowd hurried past. Fellow travelers checked the assigned compartment seats against the numbers on the yellow tickets and scampered aboard. At the same time, Mamma struggled with her passes, a large wicker basket, oversized shopping bags, several pieces of luggage—and the kids.

"Laaaas' call," hollered the conductor, "Aboooooard ..."

Chug, chug, chug. The long yellow train was on a time clock, and it wasn't going to wait for anybody! A sudden rush of panic caught me off guard as Mamma pushed me toward the hissing steam and a flight of steep, cold steps.

"This is our car," she said, panting. "Climb quickly!"

"I can't reach, Mamma."

"You have to get up those steps in a hurry!"

Her heels wobbled unsteadily as she boosted her little ones with her shoulder and suitcases.

"All abooooard!" came the same loud voice. "Las' call. All abooooard."

Irritated puffs of white steam hissed at the tardy passengers. Then, with an unexpected lurch, the strong, monstrous wheels strained to move. A fair-sized brass bell clanged with coldness and authority as the three of us scrambled to an uncomfortable set of seats on the coach.

I wanted a lengthy explanation of our impending adventure, but Mamma was puffing as she arranged the baggage, blankets, pillows, and bric-a-brac. She hoped the latter would entertain her kids on the long, long trip southward.

It had all started when the postman delivered a letter from the new chief petty officer named Daddy. Though I couldn't yet read, I knew it was from him. Like his duffel bags, the stationery smelled of gunship metal. He said he was eager to see us and regretted the ship wasn't docking at Mare Island.

"She's pulling into San Diego. I'll meet you at the train station," he wrote. "I hope you can manage things yourself. I just thought you'd like to know I'm just as in love with you as the first time I ever laid eyes on you ... and I miss you so much." Of course she could deal with the inconveniences of another long trip with the kids. Mamma was a military wife. Hadn't she always managed?

Though disheveled, she settled into her seat and did her best to create a comfortable environment for the long trip ahead. Wide-eyed, we continued to chatter, unconcerned about other less busy travelers. David finally wiggled in a cozy blanket, pulled the covers over his head, sucked his thumb, and battled heavy eyelids. Mamma stroked his hair and smiled. He looked like his father in miniature. I stared out the steamy window and rocked rhythmically as the train hurried through the foggy morning.

Occasionally, people strolled up and down the narrow aisles, passing from car to car. As doors opened and closed, blasts of cold air rushed into the sparsely furnished compartments. When the doors opened, the clickety-clacking sounds grew louder, then blended into the mumble of smartly dressed passengers. Like a row of puppets on unsteady ground, they swayed with the motion of the train. They clutched the backs of seats and passed one another cautiously; I wondered where they were going in such a slow hurry.

"Never mind," Mamma said. "Why don't you snuggle in your warm blanket and have a little rest?"

Rest? Why would she say that? I seldom napped—and when I did, it was under duress and threats of bodily harm. Frowning, Mamma said she needed to unwind. She whispered, "Nancy, you have two speeds, high and off. Let's see what we can do about a little more off!" The scabs on my knees validated her assessment. I thought life was a race, and I seemed to run from event to event at top speed.

Wiggling uncomfortably, I whispered, "I—I have to go to the bathroom."

Mamma rolled her eyes impatiently. "I know you can hold it a little longer. Wait until your Davie wakes up."

Squirming and whining, I told her I needed to go *now*. Perhaps it was the serious look on my face or the unmistakable dance that convinced her I was telling the urgent truth. Mamma sighed—relieved when a stranger's eyes met hers. The older woman smiled knowingly and said she was eager to lend a hand.

"I'll stay with your little boy while you take her to the next car," offered the stranger.

Grateful for the assistance, Mamma assured her we'd hurry. Travelers stepped aside as the gray-haired woman slid into Mamma's empty seat. "He'll be just fine," she whispered. With a wave of her hand, she smiled kindly and motioned us away.

Mamma and I passed from car to car, looking for the powder room until we finally located it. Of course, there was a line—but the look on my face and unmistakable urgency in my dance steps motivated passengers to step aside considerately.

One could never say a ride on the sleek Pacific Coaster was uneventful. It sped along the tracks like a horse heading for the barn at the end of the day. There was a reason the train had a reputation for being on time, and it was well earned.

The views of the sea from the train windows were magnificent. Like most passengers, David and I were mesmerized by the ever-changing vistas, and Mamma's endless stories entertained eavesdroppers. No one could ever say she was a novice when it came to traveling.

Boats bobbed lazily offshore as white, foamy waves washed the sandy beaches. When we weren't fidgeting on the hard, leather-lined seats, Mamma rationed tempting snacks. She was always well prepared. Storybooks and toy cars provided other temporary distractions.

Rocked by the swaying cars, we passed through small towns, farms, and vast expanses of undeveloped land. David and I were impatient to reach our final destination and reunite with the elusive sailor that belonged to us. It had been a long time since we'd seen him. I wondered if we'd remember the smiling man whose picture we kissed good night. *Oh yes*, I thought. *He's tall, and he wears a dark-colored uniform.*

The train suddenly lurched as a thin, dark man wearing a familiar-looking cap curved his way through the swaying car. He wore a meticulous uniform that almost matched his complexion. The porter stood tall, his feet anchored firmly to the floor as the car swayed from side to side. The man was pleasant, with an unusually bright smile and dark, sparkling eyes. Efficient, courteous, and friendly, it was apparent he enjoyed his work. Slowly, he strolled our way. He was busy and preoccupied with punching holes in passengers' tickets. He was an experienced worker and had answers to every concern posed by travelers. As he neared our seats, he smiled broadly.

Suddenly, I recognized the uniform. It had been some time since the sailor had been home, but the uniform was definitely … a uniform. Unable to contain my joy any longer, I lunged forward, startling the unsuspecting porter, and threw my arms tightly around his legs. Squealing loudly, I cried, "That's my daddy!"

Mamma's jaw dropped, and her face turned as red as if she'd spent the afternoon in the sun. I began to babble about waiting a long time to see him and wondering why he didn't come home sooner.

With bulging eyes, the startled man tried to unpeel himself from the happy embrace—from the hardy clutch around his long, skinny limbs. He was busy apologizing for the mistaken identity—as fast as I was busy inviting him back into our world. Fellow travelers attempted to repress their laughter at the apparent blooper, but the porter had no sense of humor. None at all. He was busy expressing his regrets to Mamma and every other grinning passenger! It was as if he were a thief caught with one hand in the cookie jar and swearing contrived innocence. Of course, I had no idea what the snickering was about or why the man was backing away so frantically. But at Mamma's insistence, I released the stranglehold on his leg and looked quizzically at the poor sweating man.

"Does this gentleman look like your daddy?" Mamma said, loud enough for all to hear.

Well, it wasn't a perfect match but close enough.

"No," she calmly explained. "This man is a porter for the railroad, and our daddy is a sailor in the navy."

"What's the difference?" I asked. "He's wearing Daddy's hat and coat ..." It took a while for the discussion to end. But Mamma had the rapt attention of every gawking person within earshot—except the worried porter who stopped clicking tickets and hightailed it out of the car as quickly as possible!

When the train finally pulled into the station at the end of the line, Daddy met us as promised. He wasn't wearing his uniform, but the unmistakable scent of the ship permeated his being. He wondered why I seemed aloof.

I looked up at Mamma and asked, "Are you sure he's my daddy?"

If Mamma said it was, it was. She did, and he was!

CHAPTER 28

The Bouncing Baby Bottle

West Oakland, California, 1947

Mamma hid it from visitors, not eager for any of her acquaintances to know her six-year-old was still savoring everything drinkable from a baby bottle. Suspicions indicated the youngster had a psychological need for the glass relic—perhaps a kid form of separation anxiety or something like that. On the common playgrounds, friends and foe alike began to whisper about the odd sight of the big kid with the baby bottle! Mamma was uncomfortable with others scrutinizing her and the child as the bottle swung happily from the big girl's teeth. It was "downright embarrassing," she said.

Peculiar, the daughter thought.

When grilled by well-meaning friends, the red-faced mother explained it was easier to dilute food, pour it into a bottle, and serve it to her child. Always on the run when the child wasn't feverish, the bottle replaced unpleasant "squabbles over chow on a fork." Regardless, it seemed the strangers' disapproving looks were taking precedence over the needs of the skinny, unhealthy little girl with a peculiar fetish. Some visitors muttered under their breath, while others simply gawked. Others superciliously raised and lowered their eyebrows.

But as often as she could, Mamma secreted the bottle facts from nosy, inquiring minds. Guests with lukewarm apathy pondered her long-suffering patience. People who knew her well understood that patience wasn't one of Mamma's virtues. What little empathy she had was wearing thin. Oh, it wasn't the bottle, per se, that was most annoying; it was the frequent, messy spills. Doing her best to placate the lonely little girl, Mamma kept a stash of absorbent cloths nearby.

The child had a history of high fevers, ear infections, and sore throats. The doctors were sure her tonsils were the probable cause. Her conditions were temporarily relieved with antibiotics, time, and blessings from church clergy. Of course, surgery would most likely be a long-term cure. But the unpredictability of ether, an unstable anesthetic at the time, was not a viable use for young children—except in cases of dire emergencies. In the meantime, Mamma did her best to appease the cranky, stubborn child and keep meddlesome contacts at bay.

When Mamma inquired at the navy hospital regarding the bottle issue, well-seasoned physicians were only slightly concerned about the possibility of psychosis. They didn't feel removing the child's security bottle was necessary just yet.

"Let's not concern ourselves with the bottle issue for now," one doctor said, thoughtfully tapping a medical chart in his hand with a pencil. "Getting the right nutrients into her system is far more important than how she does it. As long as she's ingesting her meals, I think she'll outgrow her dependency on the bottle. I wouldn't worry about it for now. Masticating is painful with ear and throat infections, and I don't like those high fevers. She's simply not interested in a fork and spoon. I'm more concerned about how thin she is. She's tall for a child of her age, and her weight continues to drop. I'll speak with my colleagues about the feasibility of lancing her eardrums and a tonsillectomy. But I need to explain, the ether is dangerous, and we don't like to use it for children's surgeries. I'll get back to you soon."

The longing for the bottle's comfort continued, as did the hole's size at the end of the rubber nipple. Unfortunately, spills and accidents also increased. Milky-thinned mush, mashed potatoes, soup, gelatins, wishy-washy concoctions—anything pulverized and diluted that could pass itself off as healthy went into the glass bottle and slowly disappeared. In an attempt to "wean her down," the bottle systematically disappeared.

"Babies need that bottle for their milk more than you do. You're a big girl now," Mamma reasoned. But it was of little use. The bottle, an extension of bliss itself, gave solace to the little soul in a world of loneliness and discomfort. The little daughter hoarded the friend like a miser, carried it under her arm, and spoke to it when nobody else was listening. The child complained bitterly when her mother put her foot down and brought out a bowl and spoon. The fretful tantrums worked miracles, and the bottle reappeared, thanks to the empathy of a grumpy, annoyed mother. The weaning process wasn't going well, nor was anybody following doctors' orders. "All right," Mamma gave in grimly, "drink—and don't spill a drop—or else!"

Of course, the occasional mishaps continued.

New rules were put in place, and Mamma enforced them like a boot camp drill sergeant. She forbade the use of it when company visited. She was adamant. The bottle was never to be seen in public places. Thus, a pseudo truce was drawn.

However, when the child wasn't slurping, and the fevers weren't raging, she tucked the bottle under her arm and carried it everywhere. She hummed quietly in a busy world of solace and kid things. Once emptied, to Mamma's chagrin, she gave in to her child, puckered her brow, and refilled it. She said the little girl and bottle seemed inseparably connected. It accompanied the child to bed at naptime. She woke up with it in the morning, and breakfast was emptied into it. She played with it, read stories with it, and, at the end of a busy day, slept with it resting safely on her pillow.

Tired, Mamma retrieved and washed the treasured glass bottle with hot, soapy water—until duty called the following morning. Sometimes she raised an eyebrow and quizzed, "Do you know any other big kids who still drink from a baby bottle?"

The youngster was tactfully silent. Some private thoughts are best left unspoken.

It was on one of those sick days that Mamma drove to the navy hospital again. Corpsmen were busy wheeling people from building to building, oblivious to all but their patients. Mother and child, bundled warmly, sat on a hard wooden bench in the hallway. awaiting their turn to be seen. When at last "Foltz" was called, Mamma trailed behind the worker with the child in tow. As they reached a small examining room, the forbidden bottle slipped unceremoniously to the floor in front of God and the entire medical staff! The little daughter had surreptitiously placed "the friend" under her warm coat.

It clattered to an abrupt halt as the knock-kneed, bare-legged child did her best to ignore unwanted attention. At last, she picked it up, thankful it didn't break, and polished off the last bit of juice.

Mamma's rules, blatantly disobeyed, had the full attention of an unfamiliar physician. He had a few unsympathetic words to say to the red-faced mother in private.

"I think it's about time for that tonsillectomy," he added finally. "We'll deal with the matter of the ether. She's probably old enough to handle it. I'll see what we can do to get her well—and trained!"

As promised, the surgery was uneventful. However, bottle dependency was another matter.

Mamma snipped another piece from the nipple to facilitate a thinly cooked cereal breakfast and handed the bottle to the child. Almost immediately, when the child used it, the nipple pulled away from the bottle. Mamma lunged at the resulting spill with a rag and glared through her wrath. Visibly upset, Mamma's endurance had spilled over the dam of tolerance for the last time.

"I promise I will never spill again," whimpered the startled little girl.

Mamma didn't want to hear why or that the cap was loose. Her hands were shaking as she bent uncomfortably close to her daughter's face covered in the milky mess. Her breath was warm, but her words were colder than the chips of ice that fell from iceman's tongs. *She was through!*

Exhaling an ominous warning, she said, "You had better be very, very, very careful, or that bottle is going to disappear faster than an iceberg in the middle of the Mojave Desert!"

The final accident was life-altering.

With the resolve of a starving piranha waiting for its next meal to swim by, Mamma grabbed the beautiful bottle and stomped to the kitchen. Flinging the window wide open, with Olympian strength, she hurled the thing high into the air. It twirled and soared past the sandbox, past the swings and slides—and suddenly disappeared.

I wanted to run after it, but Mamma guarded the back door like a snarling grizzly. Not even a giant tantrum influenced her mood for good. A terrible scene ensued. I knew the missing friend was out there, and without it, I didn't have a single friend in the world. Mamma threatened to toss me through the same window if the complaining continued.

There are times when even youngins know enough is enough. I had just experienced the first of many unforgettable experiences. Tearfully, I looked at Mamma. She stood there, red eyes blazing, bigger than apples. Defiantly, she stared back, waiting for one more excuse to explode completely.

Her apron nearly touched the floor as she bent over to face me with her hands on her hips. Quietly, she glared at me, face-to-face. Emphatically, and with unpretentious self-approval, she whispered, "Congratulations. You are permanently cured!"

She was a lot less irritable when she wasn't soppin' up kid messes. She was right when she said the bottle went to a good home, to a needier child, and I would completely forget the incident one day.

And they say I'm over it. So they say …

CHAPTER 29

Pride and Promises

West Oakland, California, 1947

At the end of World War II, new homes were going up at breakneck speed. The focus of fast and furious projects was rooted in need and occasionally greed. Money people recognized returning military people had ambitions of settling with their families in homes of their own. With visions of peaceful tomorrows, they qualified for VA home loans and redefined normalcy. New housing was the number one priority! Roads and well-planned communities with parks, stores, and schools could wait—houses, houses, houses!

It was an exciting weekend when happenstance drove the chief's family from the city to the countryside. Large billboards directed traffic to brand-new building sites as farmlands rapidly disappeared. Signs enticed happy people to live their dreams, joyfully soliciting the curious to follow the sounds of saws and hammers. Builders offered steep discounts in safer rural neighborhoods—a place where crickets rapturously sang praises day and night. Oh, the suggested plans! Private homes, privacy, backyards for barbequing, swings, and slides for the kids.

"With no money down, I think we can afford the monthly payments," Madelaine supposed. It was better than wasting it on rent. Harold hemhawed with practicality. He noted there was no assurance shore duty would grant permanence anywhere. He said a house payment wouldn't go away if another transfer came—and grinning, they signed on the dotted line. It was a happy day when the chief moved his family from the cramped apartment in Oakland to the countryside, though most homes were still under construction. The possibilities of a new life in the country were thrilling. Contractors offered steep discounts and a safer environment for learning and growing.

The paint was hardly dry as families poured into the muddy, roadless neighborhoods. "We'll be needing some playground equipment as soon as the fence is up." Of course, the builder said he'd do it. But he was really, really busy and filed the promise under "Maybe tomorrow." He didn't realize when really, really important things needed attention, Mamma was dead serious about *today*. She thought she could move mountains and was irritated with the errant builder who promised to "doze and get her yard ready for grass." She was eager to get her fence in place, as well as the yard.

But the contractor was avoiding her more and more often. He was too busy to talk, eager to get more homes on the market as fast as possible. Why, people were standing in line with their pens, ready to sign contracts! The place was a boomtown. Anxious contractors surveyed the progress, made empty promises, and waved their arms in the air, motioning heavy equipment this way and that. Tired and overworked foremen barked at harried tradesmen. Heavy equipment moved right in. Its workers were not easily distracted by complainers. Cement trucks gashed ruts in wet fields. Roads and telephone poles appeared. The sound of pounding nails was music to the contractor's ears as he sold lot after lot. Soon, there wasn't even a hint the property had ever belonged to the Castros and others who once farmed it.

It was on one of those occasions that Mamma cornered a busy, yellow-hatted foreman. When did they plan to level her lot? She pressed him for an exact date. He frowned and looked down at the tiny blond. It was apparent he misjudged her, for he was not prepared for a commitment or the fulfillment of promises she staunchly demanded.

She shouldn't have had to say she was a navy wife with two young children and a husband at sea. Nor should she have had to remind him of the small print on the contract. Anxious to get her house and yard in order, she gave orders like an admiral in an apron. And when she did, wise men moved out of her way.

The rest of the company seemed invisible to the men in charge—except for the prospective buyers standing by, listening intently to the exchange between Mamma and the builder. Mamma was an inspired leader, a doer when things needed doing. She wasn't disingenuous, and there was no ambiguity in her dealings. Her word stood for honesty, and she demanded the same from others. One always knew precisely where one stood with her. But she did have a few little quirks.

When the thoroughly irritated builder said he'd discuss the matter with her later, on her own property, the tenor of her gentle voice suddenly made crystal glasses dance on the shelves. Through with waiting and apologies, she screeched at the startled workers who promised months ago to pick up after themselves—and had no intentions or time to comply. After a quick trip to her lot, Mamma and the infuriated builder flapped their arms, bobbing heads in the air like a couple of bossy old crows. She was all the more furious when the head man stomped away, ignoring "the little woman."

"I want your messy mountain of construction crap outta my yard—*now!*"

Yelling into the wind, she stood alone on a mountain of stones, building debris, and dirt, unable to do the job herself.

The builder was too angry to argue. But nearing sunup the following morning, when birds began chirping for curious worms, the contractor answered her request. Tranquility disappeared as the outraged man noisily revved his heavy equipment outside her bedroom window. Raucously, the yellow backhoe growled at the clueless neighbors. The builder was busy granting Mamma's demands—and the mountain of junk and miscellaneous building debris disappeared.

She smiled when he left, brought out a rake, and finished a man's work. The chief would be proud of her. She wanted a picture-perfect yard the next time he had leave. And it wasn't long before a baby green lawn was sprouting. Pint-sized trees and a respectable garden appeared. She planted honeysuckle and intimidated resident gophers with her brand of patience—a ruthless pitchfork.

Needing a clothesline, she dug a couple of holes in the hard clay and mixed bags of cement in an old bucket. Who knew how long she held each post in place before the cement hardened? One by one, stateside husbands crossed clotheslines from their honey-do lists. A carpenter's daughter, Mamma was proud of her handiwork, blisters and all. Her projects made her the envy of the neighborhood.

It was a relief when her clean, wet clothes flapped regularly in the cool bay breezes. The contractor eventually moved on with his building, still frowning and trying to forget the little blond navy wife. She would not take no for an answer and never forgot a promise.

CHAPTER 30

Larry the Leaper

Castro Valley, California, 1949

Summer construction continued at an all-time high, but with fall drawing near, the need for a schoolhouse for the flood of new children was causing quite a stir. City fathers suggested, as a temporary classroom, the "Old Adobe"—a one-room Spanish-style building constructed in the mid-1800s—would make an exceptional temporary classroom for all the children of varying grade levels.

"Use it until we come up with a better idea," they proffered.

The suggestion proved to be barely tolerable. Parents dodged construction equipment and wove through dangerous, unpaved, muddy fields with no other choice but to ferry their children to the old facility. Getting safely through the construction sites was a legitimate concern.

Finally, Mamma organized a special meeting at our house, and word-of-mouth spread quickly. Our home was packed with strangers and new neighbors who chattered like old friends. All were united in their uneasiness—eager to discuss plans for decent roads, transportation, and how best to protect and educate the children. Also of concern was the lack of teachers and the need for a real schoolhouse, play equipment, and a fence for protection.

Of course, youngsters were relegated to the backyard during the meeting, instead of Mamma's clean house.

The following week, another organized meeting took place with the school board and several contractors. Every parent showed up for the discussion. The meeting turned unruly when the board insisted there was no money for a new school or even a small bus. However, they said that they were "empathetic."

Public officials raised their eyebrows as Mamma stood at the podium and emphatically declared, "Education, safety, and transportation must be everyone's immediate and highest priority."

The board curtly retorted, "The issue of transportation belongs to the parents."

The discussion went from thunderous to downright ugly. Mamma, the neighbors, and the board found themselves at an impasse. After a fruitless shouting match, the meeting adjourned, and Mamma returned home in a terrible huff.

Undaunted, she planned another neighborhood get-together and asked for suggestions for solving the pressing problems. No one had any ideas—except Mamma. She was dazzling. When she finished speaking, the unanimous conclusion was: she has the right idea! We'll find our own way to get the kids to the Old Adobe and lobby for a real school in our neighborhood.

Since no transportation was to be provided by school officials, the parents collectively opted to present their case to the decision-makers at a local taxi company—led, of course, by Mamma. Eager to get her two cents in, she was first in line. She wanted to have her say before the crowd grew too rowdy.

"Our youngsters need you," she pleaded. "It's a civic duty to provide transportation for kids to school. The school board insists they can't afford it. We want to hire you to do the job! Come up with a fair price and a bid to transport the kids on our block to the Old Adobe, and the contract is yours. You are our last and best hope." She didn't precisely disclose how many children lived on the block but felt confident a single cab (and fee) would suffice.

Mamma seldom squeaked out tears for sympathy, though she could be very persuasive in conveying herself as a poor navy wife struggling to raise a family by herself while her husband was off defending their constitutional rights, freedom as Americans, and free enterprise. Her baby-blue eyes always commanded attention. She used them as she dickered. When she was very serious, frustrated, or really wanted her way, she batted them and dickered faster than an auctioneer on stimulants.

That day in the taxi office, as witnessing heads swung from the left and right, she negotiated and bargained for the whole block. At last, it was agreed: the company would transport all the kids to the Old Adobe in one rather expensive cab, and the parents would split the fare.

The final item of business, highly crucial to Mamma, was how much would they charge? Her scarce navy dollars were already stretched to the max.

"Umm ... we'll work out something reasonable," promised the manager.

Mamma wrote the contract and gathered signatures from every family on the block. It stated the taxi would pick up the children on our street every Monday through Friday, 8:00 a.m. promptly—starting, of course, at our house at the top of the hill. They also agreed that the cabby would return as many children as he picked up that morning. When Mamma haggled with the taxi company for only one expensive fare, she neglected to inform them exactly how many passengers to expect.

I was nearly seven years old when the public taxi became our little yellow school bus. Members of the school board read about it in the local newspaper. They recognized Mamma's pointing finger right away.

On the first day of school, the driver graciously opened the back door of the cab. Naturally, I positioned myself comfortably in the middle of the seat. Mamma knew I could handle myself with the best of 'em. In her housecoat, smiling approvingly, she gently escorted little David to the front seat.

"Keep your eyes on my son. He's young, and this cab stuff is new."

The driver stopped briefly, house after house. Little passengers clamored under, over, and around the fortunate commuters who'd already selected the best seats. Other youngsters piled onto the front seat with my little brother. The rest of the children stuffed themselves into the back.

Unfortunately, the last kids to climb aboard were on their own.

The escalating situation culminated with cranky children complaining about being layered on the ledge of the back window. Others sat on laps several tiers high. The rest were relegated to the floor. The rear seat (where I once comfortably placed myself) resembled a subway station during rush hour.

Once out of Mamma's sight, the driver was definitely not a gentleman. He threatened to put several youngsters in the trunk if they didn't settle down, stop complaining, and get along. Apparently, he didn't know much about kids. Unfortunately, we taught him much more than he ever wanted to know.

I quickly surmised traveling in the packed taxi was worse than riding through the rutted mud in Mamma's old car. Her temper blazed, and she cussed as she dodged earth-moving equipment and shocked workers. I was sure riding with her was still safer than being transported in the overflowing cab.

I said, "These kids are breathing up all my air!"

Each morning, the last kid to be picked up was a well-mannered boy named Larry. He was the kindest child in the neighborhood. Unlike me, he was quiet, polite, and accommodating. He didn't want to be the last straw on the pile, but he was. He never complained. I did his share of being tetchy for him.

It was amazing the driver always found room for just one more kid in the bulging cab. Apologetically, Larry piled in. Of course, there wasn't any room for him, but the driver didn't seem to notice. He closed the door with half of Larry's skinny frame still hanging out in the thin air.

Poor Larry. He quietly managed to find a minuscule crevice among the passengers, someplace to put his little feet, his carefully packed lunch, and a book for sharing time.

On one of those ordinary but fateful taxi-stuffing mornings, Larry had the misfortune of sitting next to me.

Once Larry was inside, the driver leaned into the door, shoved it a/gainst the pile of kids, grunted it closed, and told us to make room for poor Larry. I didn't mind that he was a cooty-carrying kid, but I huffed that there was no room for him!

Even on a good day, I didn't like crowds moving into *my* space. It was uncomfortable wearing heavy coats and carrying school gear.

There was simply no wiggle room at all. Those who could reach the frosty windows scribbled nonsensical doodles on them and complained they were cold and running out of air. The driver turned up the stuffy heater.

"Larry," I complained, "just scoot over!" It didn't matter that there was no *over*. He squeezed himself awkwardly in the narrow crevice between the seat, the door, and me.

"I can't move. There's no room," Larry apologized.

"Well, why don't you just open the door? That will give all of us plenty of room," I snidely suggested.

He looked quizzically and replied, "Are you sure? Do you dare me?"

I double dared him—and he did!

We all watched in shock as Larry flew out of the cab onto the middle of the street. Perhaps it was the extra pressure in the overloaded car that propelled him so quickly. He bounced a couple of times and then was very still. It looked like he was sleeping as he lay on the pavement, bloodied and motionless. The driver screeched to a halt and dashed to the little boy in the road.

Why did I ever dare him? I thought to myself, horrified. *That was a foolish thing to do!* Then, I selfishly mused, *Well, there'll be more room for the rest of us!* I hoped he wasn't dead. We gawked out of the back window and heard the ambulance coming before we saw it.

Exasperated and shaking, the cabby tried to explain what happened, but he didn't know in truth. It was a secret that only Larry and I shared—and I certainly was not going to tell! Traumatized and frightened, I hid our secret well, but I felt sick inside. I thought to myself, p*erhaps" his baby brother might never know how kind and gentle Larry is—was.*

Of course, we were very late for school. But the principal forgave us. He extended his sincere sympathies and was terribly upset. The nurse examined each of us with extraordinary care. She asked lots of questions.

The principal queried all of us, even more so than the nurse. I carefully stayed reticent. I would not disclose my secret to anyone—not to the taxi driver, the police officers, worried parents, fellow classmates, or wary teachers.

Mamma showed up in her old Ford. She asked me some pointed questions, but my responses were vague and vaporous. Sticking to my guns, I reiterated that I didn't know what happened or why the door "got opened."

She wanted to talk about the accident and pried with uncomfortable queries. It was as if she knew I had something to hide. I didn't want to tell her anything and didn't. I didn't want to talk about Larry, the taxi, the school, or the accident. Drowning in a lake full of guilt, I felt sick and worried about my friend.

Of course, Larry didn't go to school for months. "Stay away from Larry's house," Mamma said. "He was badly injured, and his parents are worried and distraught."

I asked important questions of those who should have known how he was mending, but no one had answers—except Larry, who suffered a severe concussion and multiple broken bones. I just wanted to know he was going to be OK someday.

The accident motivated the school board to come up with immediate solutions to the school issues. The quickest: pave a street leading from our road through the construction site to the Old Adobe. Priorities changed quickly as plans for the creation of an elementary school took center stage. The new building was to be constructed two doors from our house—the first primary school in the valley.

Mamma spoke to the owners of the cab company. They were liberal regarding fees for the rest of the school year. But she knew they would have done anything to back out of the kid-transportation business if they had not signed the binding contract she had created.

No one ever knew that I was to blame for Larry's accident. It was a well-kept secret between the two of us. When Larry was finally released from the hospital, I didn't visit him very often. Truthfully, I didn't want to see what I had done. When he could converse coherently and was well enough to return to school for short visits, he proudly displayed his bandages and casts. He was recovering from injuries that could have altered or taken his life.

Larry couldn't recall what happened. Over and over, he said he had no idea what happened. Was he telling the truth? How could someone forget something as important as "the accident"? I didn't want to stare at him, but as I passed his chair, I quietly muttered, "I'm sorry."

He couldn't remember how the accident happened—but I never forgot.

The little boy was more than a neighbor and an excellent friend. In my mind, he was a hero for not dying. And who was the best secret keeper ever? It was the one and only Larry the leaper!

CHAPTER 31

Private Party

Castro Valley, California, 1950

Giddy people carried bright red valentines, boxes of cellophane-wrapped chocolates, and dime store cutouts. It was that time of year.

No, the chief would not be home for Valentine's Day or my birthday, but I had plans for a bash that would never be forgotten. I reminded neighborhood friends, casual acquaintances, total strangers, and the entire school: "The day after Valentine's Day is my birthday! I'll be nine years old."

Responses were always the same: "Are you gonna have a party?"

"Of course! What else are birthdays for?"

As more and more Valentines appeared, I sensed Mamma would soon be having a serious talk with me. We had plans to make. We had invitations to write. She was the best party organizer ever and baked our beautiful birthday cakes all by herself. She always had just the right number of candles poked securely into the icing, lit them, and initiated the singing of "Happy Birthday." She was the person to make happy birthday parties happen.

After dinner one evening, Mamma laid the newspaper aside. Sighing, she casually said, "Well, I suppose we should be making plans and a list of people to invite to your birthday party." I ran to the desk and found a thick pad of paper and a yellow pencil with a hardly used eraser.

"OK, I'm ready," I eagerly replied.

She asked for the names of people I really wanted to invite. Sitting comfortably at the kitchen table, she laboriously wrote every name I gave her. She was unusually patient—though, after a certain length of time, she raised an eyebrow and rolled her eyes. I was sure I'd listed everybody I knew, every dear friend and all the other kids I didn't know—but expected they'd bring posh, elaborate birthday presents.

Each year as my birthday rolled around, I sadly noted the-thought-that-counts Christmas gifts from the previous December were broken, lost, or tattered. There was never money for expensive, better-made presents. So, by February, I eagerly anticipated a new load of surprises from generous friends—gifts with my name on every box!

When most of Mamma's tablet pages were wholly covered with birthday names I'd carefully recited, she reminded me of the family rule, only one guest per year of our birthdays was allowed. It was a die-hard family tradition, without exceptions. That meant nine-year-old people invited only nine friends! Reluctantly and tearfully, I helped Mamma eliminate invitees. Together we performed radical surgery until only nine names remained. My brother, David, headed that precious list; Mamma put him there. To no avail, I protested, "Brothers don't count!" Of course, I wailed. Only nine kids? What about the whole school? I'd invited all of them and their teachers!

Like a wooden toy, Mamma shook her head from side to side. She knew I wasn't a big fan of sharing. Her subtle psychology was: with only nine children involved in the party games (and candy prizes), my chances of winning were much greater than if we had a yard full of covetous kids all competing for the prizes!

Her logic was indisputable, and I was finally convinced. Nine choice guests were better than a whole school of less interested guests who hardly knew me and might win the prizes.

Drying my tears, and with Mamma's help, we settled down to the vital work of party planning. We fashioned nine outstanding birthday invitations and placed them in colorful envelopes. I inscribed, in my very best penmanship, the names of each guest. Clandestinely, the messages were delivered to only eight of my most special friends, and one was held back, against my will, for brother, David. As the fourteenth of the month neared, children secretly dropped Valentine tokens into colorfully decorated mailboxes on a table in the back of the classroom. As the boxes filled and children peeked, squeals of delight seemed to override remembrances of my party.

On the long-awaited fifteenth of the month, the actual day of my birth, Mamma carefully filled paper cups with ice water and placed them on the party table in the kitchen of our small, cozy home. She said water was perfect for washing down gooey icing. I much preferred sweetened drinks, but she noted water would do.

Mamma bought colorful paper napkins and a tablecloth to match, plus nine small candles. Her acumen excelled when it came to small, intimate parties. And each year, her cakes were predictably perfect—except for the year she covered an utterly delicious cake with a mountain of ghastly shredded coconut. Fortunately, that was David's birthday, not mine. My shameful face, gagging, and other ugly sounds helped her remember which of her two kids disliked coconut. David, of course, never complained. I wondered why he was her favorite.

Anticipating the party, I daydreamed precisely where to seat each guest as I envisioned friends wearing pointed party hats and blowing rolled-up party horns.

With the skill of a civil engineer, I surveyed the backyard. Our small cement patio was perfect for playing games.

Dangling honeysuckle vines made a spectacular canopy, thanks to Mamma's beloved father, a skilled carpenter and a gardener. When the covering was in place, he was sure his handiwork was just what she ordered. "Daughter dear," he said, "are you sure you want me to plant honeysuckle? You'll have a shady covering, but it will attract every bee in the valley."

She was, he did, and the bees loved it.

Early in the morning, before guests arrived, Mamma reminded me to dust the phonograph. "We'll need it for musical chairs," she mused.

It was difficult to slide the kitchen table out the back door. Mamma said kids eating cake and ice cream was an outdoor activity. I knew what that meant—no running in the house and no spilling. The party guests were expected to use their best manners.

I visualized the cake exactly in the middle of the table, right in front of me. I told Mamma it was going to be a tight fit for all the kids and expected presents! Rolling her eyes, she said, "Don't worry. We'll make room for everything—kids, presents, and all!" It was a relief to have that concern taken off my shoulders. I imagined pretty boxes and colorful cards with my name on every one of them. I envisioned what the guests might bring: jewelry, games, a jump rope, jacks, new crayons, or perhaps a coveted journal or autograph book! The joyous anticipation was unbearable.

Nancy Ann lived across the street. She was my very best friend, most of the time—full of secrets and good ideas. We whispered incessantly about the party. But no amount of coaxing could weasel out of her what special gift she planned to bring. I was sure it was going to be significant, exciting, and extraordinarily impressive. She said on Saturday afternoon, the day of my birthday, she'd skip across the street to my house for the two o'clock celebration.

Unfortunately, a few days before the big day, Nancy and I had a huge fight. The issue wasn't significant, but I was sure it was all her fault. She yelled that I was to blame. Furious, I demanded the return of my invitation. Summarily, I uninvited her to my party. I told her she was not welcome at my house—ever.

That made her livid. The angrier she grew, the louder I yelled. At an impasse, we stopped talking. We didn't walk to school or eat lunch together and glared across the classroom, making faces at each other. I didn't cooperate on the swings or even care when she fell and skinned her knee. I didn't go to the nurse's office with her or acknowledge the dressing she timidly sported. Painfully, she limped to the classroom, and I didn't help her one bit. I was completely unconcerned about my ex-friend, Nancy Ann. Even worse, I didn't care that I didn't care.

Mamma and Nancy's mother were neighborhood friends. I knew I'd hear about Nancy Ann's accident from Mamma, who, of course, would be informed by Nancy's mother. Neither mother seemed to be too concerned about the sudden stony wall of silence that stood coldly between Nancy's house and ours. "Just a little spat," one of them said. The other agreed. "The girls will work it out."

Early Saturday morning, the day of my party, Mamma assigned cleaning chores. Of course, I protested.

"It's your birthday," she quietly replied. "You're responsible for getting things ready." Handing me a dusting cloth, as she always did, Mamma said if we listened quietly to the opera on the radio, the work would go faster.

During intermission, she asked if I could play "Happy Birthday" on the piano.

"Everyone can play 'Happy Birthday,'" I replied.

It was my birthday, and I wanted to sit regally, smiling, and honored in the glow of nine pink candles, listening, not playing as each guest loudly sang, "Happy birthday, dear Nancy, happy birthday to you!"

Mamma said she didn't know how to play the song. She was going to ask me to teach her, but I didn't have time. I guessed my friends would have to sing like they always did: a cappella con gusto.

At the party's appointed hour, the house smelled of a freshly baked and beautifully decorated cake. Her creation was stunning—covered with mounds of pale pink icing. She poked small candles into it and continued to place cubes of ice into the party cups. She did it all for my birthday party. She even bought tricolored ice cream. Looking at it made my mouth water. I was still hoping she might consider a sugary drink for the auspicious occasion, but she didn't. Other kids drank pitchers of it—but not at our house. Mamma said it made holes in our teeth, and going to the dental office was a luxury we couldn't afford. Water was a far better choice, she reasoned. Nine colorful paper cups and matching plates decorated the table. The floating cubes added personality to the beverage.

One by one, friends arrived with cards and colorfully wrapped boxes. Graciously, I placed the presents conspicuously around the cake. Dressed in Sunday best, guests and I jumped in joyful glee. David, usually quiet and obedient, took his thumb out of his mouth and pointed to the beautifully wrapped gifts. My silent glare threatened him. I was his only sister, but I was not his favorite. I made sure of it.

Mamma waited patiently for all the guests to arrive before starting the games. As time passed, I was getting antsy. The cake, the kids, and the presents were exciting. "We should start pin-the-tail-on-the-donkey," I suggested.

"Not yet," she said. Glancing at her small gold wristwatch, she paced in front of the living room window. She was stalling.

"Maybe we should start musical chairs," I added.

Sensitive to her intuition, Mamma conspicuously counted and recounted noses. Then, with the wit of a wizard, she said, "Nancy Ann isn't here yet. I wonder why she's so late." Pulling the curtain aside, she peered through the window at our neighbor's quiet house.

Following her, I looked nervously across the street. It was as if looking long enough or often enough would cause Nancy Ann to come bouncing out her front door with my big, well-deserved present! I didn't want her at my party, but thoughts of a substantial gift caused me to imagine we could get along for one birthday afternoon.

Mamma said she knew Nancy's family was home. She saw someone working in the yard. Suspiciously, she asked if I'd delivered her invitation. She was sure Nancy Ann's name was on the guest list. Mumbling, I didn't say a word about uninviting her. But since she helped me write the invitations, Mamma knew precisely how many noses to count. Just that morning, she arranged a chair for every guest. She knew only one child was missing: Nancy Ann. "I think we should wait a little longer," Mamma said. "Maybe she's forgotten what time the party starts. She'll be here soon. We'll wait!"

In silence, the puzzled guests glanced uneasily at one another. Wide-eyed, I quietly confessed that Nancy Ann was not coming to my party.

"Why not?" Mamma asked.

Lying to her was insane. We both knew I wasn't good at it. She always uncovered the truth, regardless of who said what.

Excusing ourselves, Mamma led me to her bedroom and closed the door for a private tête-à-tête. She repeated her question several times and waited for an explanation. The silence was deafening.

Finally, I just blurted it out. "She's not coming 'cause I uninvited her."

"You what?"

Justifying my actions, I continued, "She hasn't been very nice to me, and I don't like her anymore. I told her to stay home!"

"But she lives right across the street, and you two are best friends.

She invited you to her birthday party. Nancy Ann is a very nice little girl. She deserves to come to your party! You've hurt her feelings!"

I insisted Nancy Ann did not deserve any birthday cake, nor did I want her in our house. Mamma was shocked when I said, "Nancy Ann is not nice, and I don't ever want her at any of my birthday parties!"

"That will not do," Mamma informed me. "There will be *no* party until Nancy Ann is here!" Mamma wanted me to walk across the street and get her. Imagine that! She wanted me to apologize even though Nancy Ann had behaved poorly.

Shocked, I repeated Mamma's words, "That just will not do!"

Her eyes grew larger than fifty-cent pieces. Speechless, she furrowed her brow. Resolve was plastered all over her face. I knew she was not backing down. Oddly, thoughts of the cat who lived next door came to mind. When the hair on its back stood up, I knew enough was enough. Mamma reminded me of the cat. I didn't want to see if she had hair on her back or not, but I was sure it was standing straight up if she did.

Embarrassed, I had no idea what my guests would think of the tense situation. Mamma didn't care. She held my arm tightly and headed for the front door. From the windows, curious onlookers watched as we strutted across the street. Over her shoulder, Mamma explained, "We'll be right back. Don't touch the cake!" Nobody did.

We marched directly to Nancy Ann's house, where Mamma rang the doorbell and smiled. She said all the children were waiting, and we'd begin the party when Nancy Ann was ready. Mamma wanted to know if, by chance, Nancy had misplaced the invitation or forgotten what day it was. Was she ill or planning to attend later in the afternoon? With both eyebrows lifted, Nancy's mother looked down at me, muttered something under her breath, and disappeared into her house, leaving her door wide open.

It was shocking when she reappeared with my former friend. Nancy Ann's hair was beautiful with curls and ribbons. But her eyes were red and swollen, and her cheeks flushed. Her beautiful dress had wrinkles in it. Mamma, sensing the big picture, spoke directly to Nancy Ann. She said I had something to say to her.

I said it.

Again, Mamma assured the neighbors we were waiting for Nancy

Ann to arrive before starting the party. She said we wouldn't begin the games until Nancy arrived. Mamma bent down, eye to eye with the pretty little girl, and said, "All the children are waiting for you, Nancy Ann." The child's cold mother didn't even attempt to smile, but she said they would be over momentarily. Mamma smiled at the disappointed youngster and said we would be waiting.

The gawking guests were glued to the living room window, watching, and full of questions from our house. After the dramatic encounter, I wasn't very jovial. When Mamma marched me home, the curious friends kept asking about Nancy Ann. They wanted to know if she was sick. Trying to find a seed of composure, I muttered something about starting the birthday party when she arrived.

"How come she's so late?" they asked. I didn't want to tell them.

"She's almost here," I mumbled. When the doorbell rang, all the guests hurried to greet the last guest. I wasn't expecting Nancy's mother to accompany her daughter to the party, but she did. Standing on our front porch, she sternly announced Nancy Ann was happy to be invited to the birthday party! Grim-faced, her mother looked straight at me and quietly alleged she had something to say to me later.

I looked at my friend's red, swollen face, at her quivering hands and the beautifully wrapped box, tied with soft pink satin ribbons. She held it tightly and bowed her head. The present itself was suddenly not that important.

Quietly and caringly, Nancy Ann whispered, "I'm sorry we had a big fight."

I felt Mamma's knees nudge my backside. "I'm sorry we had a big fight too," I replied.

I stood there, looking at my shiny Sunday shoes as the other children wondered what was going on. I was thinking of Nancy Ann. Forgetting the other guests, it was as if Nancy Ann and I were the only two people in the room. Her mother opened the screen door and invited herself into our tidy living room. She said she couldn't stay but reassured me she would return to escort her daughter home when the party was over.

Oblivious to what had just taken place, the guests jumped with excitement. "We missed you," they said to my sorrowful friend, "and we're glad you are finally here so we can start the fun all over! We needed you at the party so we could eat the cake and ice cream. Our ice cubes are melting! We saved a chair for you, right next to Nancy Lee. Can we eat now?"

It took a little while for Nancy Ann to smile. The cake helped. I watched her mouth as she sang, "Happy birthday toooo you!" We giggled, trying to inflate the thick, colored party balloons for the next game. Nancy Ann's face was red again. We laughed at how funny she looked in the pointed party hat. She laughed back. I had never noticed how sweet her smile was.

I do not recall what treasure was in her carefully wrapped birthday box, but she beamed when she saw me open it. I smiled back and thanked her. Suddenly the gift was not very important, but I was overjoyed to get it.

At nine years of age, I learned a valuable lesson about friends, loyalties, and a forgiving heart. Realizing that a friend is worth more than any present in a box, no matter how carefully chosen or beautifully wrapped, was the present I never forgot. My keepsake was a little friend with big tears, a forgiving heart, and a bright smile. She was the friend who quickly forgave an unfortunate slight by someone who learned from her that sensitivity is a treasured gift. Through the years, she will always be remembered as the gift I never forgot.

CHAPTER 32

Mamma and the Met

(With Dusty Undertones)

"Welcome to another broadcast from the Metropolitan Opera House coming to you from Grand Central Station in New York City!"

The cheerful voice on the radio invited all to join him at the Met. The representative might as well have offered an invitation for tea and crumpets at the royal palace in England. It simply wasn't going to happen. But I convinced myself there must be a real Metropolitan Opera House somewhere in the city. I quizzed Mamma, hoping to learn more. Her answers were always the same: "Shh. Just listen and keep dusting!"

In our home, almost everything noteworthy happened on Saturdays. Mamma was up early, cleaning and vacuuming in her nightgown. By ten o'clock, we were down to straightening books, tossing old newspapers, and listening intently to the voice emanating from the large wooden box.

Mamma's homemaking training started early. It included endless hours of dusting every Saturday morning. Week after week, I polished oriental treasures and repolished them. Of course, I griped! Dust, dust, dust!

Mamma always kept a spotless home. When my work passed inspection, I was free to romp and play outside in the California sunshine. Her Saturday regimen was as predictable as milk of magnesia. She twisted the knob on the radio to find the right station, and I tackled a fresh batch of dust—best described as mysterious, unwanted particles of a substance that strews itself anywhere it pleases.

Really! Would it have mattered if I had just once let it be? Each Saturday, Mamma and I repeated the same routine: music and dust. Dust and music. Mamma insisted that dusting was my job, and with the chief at sea, she needed all the help she could get. David's assignment was more straightforward: pick up your toys, and beat it.

During a predictable dusting session, engrossed with the magic of the Met, I wondered why she bought the unusual Chinese dragons in the first place. Indeed, the carver had no idea how time-consuming it would be to dust each carefully chiseled scale. I hefted an exquisite, cold, and prized jade carving. The precious rock was heavy, and my hands were slippery with polishing oil. To my horror, the sculpture slipped from my grasp, fell to the floor, and broke. Mamma looked at me, speechless and pale.

Before leaving China, Mamma had carefully packed a large box with beautiful, expensive jade, wooden carvings, and other intricate pieces of Oriental art. She especially treasured the dragons, water buffalo, and Buddhas. After her unfortunate injury abroad, Mamma was easy prey for greedy non-Chinese workers in the Customs Office. They picked through everything she'd packed for delivery just beyond the Golden Gate, and they absconded with the more significant pieces of her collection. Each surviving item at departure had a great deal of sentimentally attached to it. Each had its own story and precious memories.

Learning the story and history of the fractured object was a painful lesson. I had not understood the emotional value placed on her trove. Of course, it was an accident, but the jade was irreparably ruined. The lesson learned was one might not put the same significance on other people's treasures, but great care and caution in handling them are paramount. The shock on Mamma's face said it all, and I never forgot I was responsible for damaging something of significant importance to someone I loved.

I asked about the smiling person with the outlandish abdomen. She said his name was Buddha, and all who rubbed his belly would enjoy good luck.

I did; he didn't. The carving was beautiful, but my Saturday luck didn't change. He simply grinned and grew dustier throughout the week. Staring into his ivory eyes, I was confident he'd reward my efforts, but he never did. His purpose seemed to be collecting dust and being the bearer of happy thoughts and smiles.

On one such occasion, I hoped my work would pass inspection before the end of the second act at the Met because friends were waiting outside to play. I wanted to fold the oily rags and bid the altos goodbye. Mamma was pleased with a clean and dustless house. Gleefully, I anticipated hearing her say, "Run along and play." But, with little or no Buddha luck, she frowned, and I continued to dust, dust, and re-dust. She had the eyes of a detective and exceptionally high standards.

"Just do it!" She frowned. And I did—every Saturday morning as we listened intently to the music from the Met. I was too busy to ever really know if such things as New York City or the Opera House truly existed. But I was convinced the cheerful voice in the radio thought it did. More importantly, Mamma knew it, and that was good enough for me.

"Good afternoon, ladies and gentlemen, and welcome to another broadcast from …" I occasionally moaned. But somehow dusting and the opera seemed to go hand in hand. The cheerfulness of the well-rehearsed voice assured dusters everywhere we were in for another exciting performance, Brunhilda and all. If it weren't for time and Scheherazade, dusting would most likely have filled the world with gritty boredom. Who knew monotonous chores and music would become the best of friends? We were predictable, working silently to create a tidy world—at precisely ten o'clock every Saturday morning.

Music works wonders. I know, because it happened one fine day!

CHAPTER 33

The Hill to Hell

Castro Valley, California, 1948

"Honey, the ship's comin' into Mare Island, and it looks like I'll be home for Christmas! We'll talk about them bikes ..."

When the mailman delivered the letter, she was giddy with plans for the best holiday ever. The most exceptional presents always arrived for my birthday or in December, or so Mamma said. However, it was no secret—Christmas belonged to the chief. How he relished it!

Decorating the tree was his domain (without kid help), as was shopping, planning, caroling, yule logs, rum-soaked fruitcakes, frothy eggnog, turkey dinners, molasses cookies, stringing popcorn and cranberries, and most of all, Mamma's famous fudge.

The chief was rarely home for the holidays. When he was, Mamma had little trouble transferring the entire holiday rituals into his capable hands. One might have thought it was his birthday. He was a child again, decorating missed trees with bright, shiny tinsel, tying up loose ends with pretty ribbons, and the warmth of home. Seeing the tree, Hal slipped into his private world, humming to the accompaniment of crackling logs in the fireplace. It was magical.

But he didn't share well. Judiciously, he guarded every string of lights, glass balls, and miscellaneous ornaments—insisting, "Kids break things." He told us to step aside and let him take over. Vigorously, he whipped Ivory soap flakes until they resembled fluffy white snow and dabbed it onto the branches of the sweet-smelling pine. As he worked, he muttered something about winters in Ohio when he was a little boy. Ohio was a mystery, and who imagined the chief was ever a little boy? Yes, Christmastime was his holiday, and Mamma did all she could to make it bright and merry.

David and I spoke of little else but bicycles. We'd been priming the pump for months.

"Oh! I wish we could afford a couple of them for you," Mamma lamented, "but having your father home is the best present of all!" And so we observed the stranger who delighted her and waited patiently for the magical Christmas morning to arrive.

The sun was barely yawning when our eyes flew open. Dashing to the beautifully decorated tree, we were thrilled to find a pair of shiny red bikes waiting to be broken in. Happy squeals summoned two sleepy parents, still rubbing their eyes. They were as "surprised" by the bikes as we were!

In his footed pajamas, David was laughing and already attempting to whiz through the house on the bike. He was doing his best to avoid the walls. My bicycle, a Schwinn "twiller" (two-wheeler), was precisely what I'd been praying for: a big girl's bike complete with a set of training wheels to hold it steady.

Gingerly, I sat on it and panicked at the shaky movement. I was sure I could learn to ride it. The chief said he would teach me—right after breakfast. David and I were far too excited to eat. What were they thinking? Breakfast could wait; riding couldn't.

Eagerly, I dressed and carefully maneuvered the new bicycle into the yard. Though I wasn't the only kid on the street with a new bike, I was undoubtedly the most enthusiastic. The excitement was contagious. Standing on the golden winter lawn Mamma had worked so hard to plant in the chief's absence, she listened attentively as he explained the uncomplicated techniques of balance and motion. The training wheels' security was a confidence booster, and with minimal scrapes, I maneuvered the bike down the hill.

"You don't need them training wheels," the chief said. "Let's take 'em off." He was convinced I was ready to solo on my own. It was reassuring to know I didn't need the trainers after all. He suggested that I "point the bike down the hill and just take off a couple of times."

Holding my breath, bolstered by his confidence, I wobbled until my own self-assurance kicked in. Before long, the wind was whipping through my hair, and I shrieked, "I can do it!"

It was exhilarating. The chief jumped up and down, clapping and cheering. He knew I could ride that bike, and more importantly, I knew I could do it.

Pedaling as fast as his little legs would go, David tried to keep up. It was no use; I was at the bottom of the hill quicker than a swarm of bees anticipating a garden of roses in bloom. David and I chattered as we walked our bikes to the rise at the top of the hill—and did it again.

"Get back on those bikes and ride! It'll make your legs stronger."

All afternoon, we whizzed up and down the road, honing our newly acquired skills. The chief was delighted with his teaching abilities and hurried into the house to share the good news. Mamma was still drying her hands on a kitchen towel when she came outside to check our progress.

"You're doing just fine!" she proudly exclaimed.

"It's really easy, Mamma. Just get on, hang on and wheeeeeeeeeee."

She proudly noted I was riding without training wheels. Did I need them? The chief guessed Santa had forgotten how big I was getting. After all, he saw us only once a year.

Mamma's interest in the bikes was noticeable.

"Did you have a bike when you were a kid?" asked the chief.

"Oh, no! We never had the money," she replied. "With such a large family, nobody had bicycles. We walked or took the bus."

"Well," said the chief, "we have bikes now. Get on. I'll teach you to ride!"

"You think I can do it?"

Cautiously, she pondered the idea. The chief said the bike was the perfect size for her. Grinning, she said, "Do you think I could get hurt trying to ride this thing?"

Walking her to the bike, he fast-paced her through the lecture on handlebars, pedals, breaks, and general safety measures. Pedal backward to control the speed, and the bike will slow down, he said. He honked the polished chrome horn, adjusted the seat, patted it, and suggested she give it a try!

Warily, she followed his lead—brave for someone who'd never, ever balanced herself on the seat of anything but a dining room chair.

She was just trying to get comfortable with the idea when the chief made a colossal blunder. Though he'd survived dangerously close encounters at sea, never in his wildest dreams did he imagine the supreme risk he took that day. He encouraged Mamma to wobble to the top of the hill on the unfamiliar bike without training wheels. He held it as she struggled, and in a moment of complete madness, he pushed her and the bike downhill, applauding as it stayed upright.

Cupping his hands, the chief bellowed, "It's just like swimming, honey! Once you get the hang of it, you can do it forever! Keep riding!"

Totally out of control, she roared in absolute terror. Her mouth and eyes flew open as she sped on the wobbly bicycle down the steepest hill in the neighborhood! It was a red blur.

"*Harold!* Harold! Harold! H-A-R-O-L-D … *make it stop*! I'm gonna *kill* ya for this! #%$&^(@&#$@!"

The chief cupped his hands over his mouth and shouted as she plowed forward, "Put on your breaks! Your *brakes … your brakes*! Do it now!"

"What *brakes*?" she bellowed at the top of her lungs. It was no use.

The wind was rushing in her ears as terror widened her eyes. The quivering wheels twisted and turned. It was easy to see the teetering pupil was scared stiff and a hundred and fifty miles past upset. Screaming, she flew full bore down the hill, doing her best to avoid parked cars, kids, neighborhood dogs, and every other darn fool thing in her way.

The bike finally ran out of steam and fell over as her family sprinted pell-mell down the hill, hoping she'd survived. Crumpled over the bike, she was clearly in shock but recovering fast. Her knees and face were skinned and bleeding. But even worse, her dignity was spread all over the street, and her pride was outlandishly gouged.

Holding his head with both hands, the chief let out a yell and sprinted to render sympathetic assistance to his fledgling pupil. What was he thinking? The look on his face spoke volumes. It was just a moment of insanely lousy judgment, he supposed. Riding a bike, he confessed, was nothing like swimming!

That was Mamma's only riding lesson. Loud enough for angels to hear, she fired her coach on the spot!

The hullabaloo caused quite a stir. Mr. Jac and his wife, the Snoots family, Miss Ann, and other neighbors rushed to Mamma's aid. It would seem she ran out of bad words shortly after she hit the ground in front of a large crowd of gawking, nervous neighbors.

The chief was so, so sorry. Awkwardly, he straightened her floral printed dress and attempted to cover her modesty. Very slowly, he picked her up and brushed her off. Then, checking for broken bones, additional scrapes, and contusions, moved by her tears, he carried her home in his arms. As he closed the door, she tapped into another reservoir of swear words and fury.

Sympathetic neighbors pushed the slightly scratched but otherwise intact Christmas bicycle up the hill and into our yard. Mamma limped to the front door with a cold compress on her head and did her best to control her tongue. She thanked them for their help and concern. In shock, Mamma momentarily forgot how angry she was. But once the door closed, she remembered.

Of course, the chief was terribly upset. Perhaps months at sea weren't so bad after all.

"Dona," Mamma later told her youngest sister, "that was my first and only bike-riding experience!" Nostalgically, she reminisced, "It was a hill to hell!"

CHAPTER 34

Sally Sue Snoots

Sally Sue Snoots was almost an invisible kid. Like our other playmate, Nancy Ann, she lived across the street too. Sally was slightly chunky, quite dull, and good company for her mother. I found her oddly intriguing. Occasionally, on cloudy days, I knocked on the Snoots' door to see if their daughter wanted to play. Mrs. Snoots always answered, dressed in the same well-worn housecoat. Most often, her reply to my question was: "What do *you* want to play?" I stammered and wondered about that myself!

Every morning, I walked or rode my bike to school with Nancy Ann. Sally never joined us. I never saw her at school. She must have been special because the school came to her. Now and then, I noted my disquieting friend watching me from her bedroom window. Her upstairs room was above a small garage, filled with chicken paraphernalia. Sometimes, through her locked window, she moved the curtain aside and waved. Sometimes she didn't. After school, she watched my friends and me play in the quiet street in front of her house, but she never joined us.

Sally Sue was a young girl, or so she appeared to be youthful. Her mother was Sally's primary source of companionship. They rarely left their house for any reason. Indeed, Sally never played outside with the rest of the neighborhood kids. Like Sally, her mother was very different. Mrs. Snoots redefined the gist of average. She never wore lipstick or used any other kind of face-enhancing potions. Her hair was mousy gray/brown, and her feet were massive and gnarled. I was fascinated by several large, unappealing warts on her face. I told Mamma about them and asked how they came to be. Frowning, Mamma said it wasn't nice to look at them.

"Don't stare," she said.

I tried not to look, but I analyzed them like a scientist when I was sure nobody was watching. Though Mrs. Snoots's eyes were tiny, she covered them with thick, horn-rimmed glasses. I was sure she could see *everything*! Most of the time, her unbrushed hair hung limply on her stooping shoulders. It gave the appearance of a much older woman. I supposed she couldn't have been that old because her daughter was close to my age. But Mrs. Snoots gave the impression of being much older than my grandmother. I never told her. Perhaps she already knew.

The Snoots moved into the house next door to Mr. Jack and his wife. The two next-door families never visited. It seemed they went out of their way to steer clear of one another. Neighbors frequently chitchatted with other families on the block, except with Sally Sue and her mother.

Mr. Jack told Mamma he was not fond of the prized chickens the Snoots were raising. Only a small fence separated his property from the chicken lovers. Since Mr. Jack frequently barbequed on his built-in brick grill, he rolled his eyes and silently complained about the flies and poop smells. They were more than an annoyance. It would appear, so were the Snoots. But Mrs. Snoots was incredibly proud of the ribbons and trophies her chicks won in various poultry competitions.

One summer afternoon, to our surprise, the Snoots invited David and me to accompany them to the county fair. The trip, with a carload of chickens pooping in their little pens, was unforgettable. David, trying not to gag, looked at me with tears in his eyes. Though he didn't say a word, I was sure the cause was chicken stink. I tried not to talk or even open my mouth to answer questions Sally Sue's mother gaily asked. I shook my head yes or no and dabbed at my own watering eyes.

Once we arrived at the fairgrounds, all the Snoots wanted to see was the poultry barns—dozens of them. David and I were not fond of the flies or the reek of the colorful poultry. But the Snoots never seemed to mind at all. Perhaps the long, confining barns—full of cackling birds—excited them in anticipation of receiving the red, blue, and gold-colored prize ribbons.

In their own small home, the Snoots placed lighted crates of chickens in their ramshackle, undersized kitchen. The house smelled of cramped cages. Mrs. Snoots raved about how beautiful her chickens were. She held them to her warted chin and babbled. She bathed them in the kitchen sink alongside stacks of unwashed dishes. The drenched creatures shivered pathetically. But holding them tenderly, Mrs. Snoots jabbered unintelligently, kissed their little yellow beaks, and wrapped the pint-sized peepers in frayed towels to dry.

She didn't visit with the neighbors as Mamma did. Maybe it was the fly thing. She just stayed in her quiet house with Sally Sue and the chicks. But several times a week, I watched as Mrs. Snoots got into her car and drove away. I could tell she was going somewhere special. Her mousy hair was twisted tightly into a bun at the back of her head. She had carefully wrapped several plastic flowers around it and smeared a little oil of some sort on her lips. Though she never wore any kind of makeup, on those special occasions, her lips looked greasy. I hoped it wasn't leftover dinner. She seemed pleased to have someplace special to go. Occasionally, Sally joined her. Sometimes she didn't. Curiosity was getting the best of me. I wanted to know where Mrs. Snoots went in the evenings and why she primped.

Unlike the Snoots household, at eventide, Mamma fed and put us to bed before the sun began to yawn. She said she needed the rest. The long, long day had passed too slowly for her. It's only six o'clock, chimed the old clock on the mantel. Mamma pulled down the bedroom shades and promised it would soon be dark outside.

David and I read storybooks, recited made-up stories, and sang songs from our wooden twin beds until we ran out of noise. "Cruising down the River," "Row, Row, Row Your Boat," and "Down in the Valley" were Mamma's favorites. When our voices were at an all-time crescendo, we sang in two-part harmony. We were magnificent! Mamma never tired of hearing us sing from our shared little room.

Little David's bed was piled with toy cars and yellow trucks. When he was tired enough, with his precious toys comfortably tucked on and under the warm blankets, he leaned on them with his pale arms extended, like a mamma chick, and slumbered. He was angelic when he was sleeping.

Things were different in the Snoots household.

"Sally Sue," I said on one of those curious occasions, "where does your mother go in her car at night?"

"Why do you want to know?" she asked. The Snoots were very, very private people. They didn't discuss their personal business or interest, except for the chickens.

"Well, I just want to know," I said.

"I'll ask my mother," Sally Sue replied. That was the end of that. She wasn't going to tell me. The more she didn't tell me, the more I wanted to know. Mamma said the Snoots were "different" people. I didn't know what she meant. Mrs. Snoot was odd, but I wouldn't call her strange. Strange was the old man three houses down who used an elephant gun to shoot our neighbor in the fourth house. With a new baby, she frequently draped fluffy white diapers over the clothesline. She told Mamma our neighbor in the third house from ours sat on his back porch, rocked, and stared at her. No one knew he was listening to strange voices in his head. He said his neighbor put a hex on him. Fortunately, the bullet barely grazed the young mother, frightening her half to death. When police officers hauled him away, he was still ranting.

No, Mrs. Snoots was not that kind of strange. But she was definitely ... out of the ordinary.

One dreary Saturday afternoon, I rang Sally Sue's doorbell. Mrs. Snoots answered. She said she'd see if her daughter wanted to play. Then pausing, she cocked her head and said, "What do you want to play?" I didn't have an answer. I hadn't thought that far ahead.

"Well," she said, "come in and think about it."

Sally Sue was glad to have company. She lived a very dull life. Rarely was her monotony interrupted, except for the chickens. Life just sort of came to pass, and on a good day, Sally Sue stepped into it.

She invited me to join her in her room to play with her toys. The room was cluttered and smelled.

"Let's clean up your room and surprise your mother," I proposed.

Sally Sue raised one eyebrow and replied, "Why?"

I didn't have a right answer, and I was beginning to wonder why I'd even bothered to ring her doorbell.

"Follow me," Sally Sue said, beaming, "and be very quiet! Don't say a word!"

Tiptoeing down her wooden stairs, past her sleeping mother, we followed our noses to the messy kitchen. I whispered, "We could clean up this mess and surprise your mother!" Sally Sue frowned. She had a better idea, she said.

On the top of the kitchen stove among the dirty pots and pans, Sally's eyes lighted upon a freshly baked cake with buttery lemon-colored frosting. She picked up the entire cake and motioned for me to follow her. Tiptoeing slowly past her snoring mother, we were quieter than two mice. With my heart pounding, we continued up the wooden steps to her bedroom. She silently closed the door and sat on the littered floor with the cake—a whole cake—in her bedroom.

"Come on," she said.

I looked at Sally Sue in disbelief.

"What are you doing?"

She gazed at me quizzically and replied she was going to eat the cake. With her unwashed fingers, she dipped into the frosting and licked them. I was stunned. I'd never even entertained the idea of touching one of Mamma's cakes. And I'd never seen anyone eat as she did, with dirty hands. Mamma made us wash and wash and wash. The idea of ruining a delicious cake was unacceptably naughty. I didn't eat a bite of it. Wide-eyed, I watched in stunned silence as she ate not only the icing but most of the cake with her bare hands. She was a mess, and she didn't even care! Shocked, I watched her hide the ugly remains under her bed.

"I need to go home," I told her.

"Why?" she asked.

"My mother will be looking for me," I fibbed.

"Well, you'll need to tiptoe very quietly to the front door—and don't wake up my mother. She's sleeping soundly. She would not want you to wake her up."

I couldn't wait to leave the Snoots' house.

"I'm never coming back here to play!" I told myself ... but I did.

I told Mamma about the cake and Sally Sue's strange behavior. For once, she listened intently.

"She took the whole cake to her bedroom, ate most of it, and hid the rest of it under her bed! Isn't that strange, Mamma? Why did she do that? Mrs. Snoots will awaken, and she might think I took her yellow cake!"

"I really don't like you playing with Sally," Mother warned. "There's something not normal about that youngster."

I didn't understand the cake thing. Mrs. Snoots never asked about it. Maybe she forgot she'd baked it, but I never did.

I continued to watch Mrs. Snoots drive off in the evenings. I tried not to notice, and I did my best to ignore Sally Sue when she waved at me from her bedroom window. Sally Sue was as odd as her mother. Neither of them seemed to notice the oddity of the other. I suppose that was a blessing.

To my shock, one day, Sally and her mother rang our doorbell. Sally was very excited and could hardly talk. She extended an invitation for me to attend summer camp with her.

Summer camp? I'd never heard of such a thing. We didn't go to summer camps. We rode bikes, ran through the sprinklers, ate picnic lunches in the backyard, and picked berries. Mamma never once mentioned summer camp. I wondered what I'd been missing. It had to be very extraordinary for Mrs. Snoots and her daughter to leave their house, cross the street, and knock on our door. It was the first time I'd ever seen Sally so animated. She wasn't even that excited about stealing the warm cake from her mother's kitchen.

I took a brochure from Sally. Not surprisingly, her mother never took her eyes off us, nor did she smile. I don't think she knew how. When they left, I handed the paper to Mamma. Quietly, her eyes slid over the words.

"What is it, Mamma?" I asked. It was an invitation to attend a church youth summer camp. She said she'd think about it. Mrs. Snoots invited me to meet the camp counselors and said they'd tell me all about the trip.

Mamma said she was still thinking.

Later that week, with both eyebrows raised, she agreed to let me go with the Snoots to meet the youth counselors. Mrs. Snoots said they were eager to meet Sally's friend. I wondered why. Considering how eccentric the Snoots family was, I had second thoughts about meeting the new people, but curiosity got the best of me. Mamma allowed me to accompany Sally and her mother to the next meeting.

Mrs. Snoots introduced me to the minister. He wanted to know if I was saved.

"Saved? From what?" I innocently inquired.

The question was a very, very big deal to the Snoots and other congregants. Backing away from my naively wicked response, the minister nearly fell into an open font of water. Red-faced, he told me I was on the road to hell. Looking slightly confused, I wondered if that had anything to do with the Snoots' peculiarities.

"Well, we'll see what we can do about gettin' you saved at summer camp," he continued.

Unsure of his meaning, I decided not to bring the issue to Mamma's attention.

"Yep," he said. "Summer camp is a *very* good idea."

Campers were required to attend lots of church meetings. After the singing and clapping, the talk turned to the camp meeting. So that was where Mrs. Snoots went in the evenings. Church in the middle of the week? Occasionally we attended church but always on Sunday mornings. Mamma said it wasn't a good idea to become too involved in the Snoots' activities. Though we rarely participated, we had our own church meetings, she said.

"They're very nice people," I assured her. "Why don't you come and see?"

I learned new songs that made Mamma frown. She didn't like the clapping or the hallelujahs. She was having second thoughts about letting me go. I decided not to reveal the minister's remarks about being a heathen and going to hell.

Mrs. Snoots assured Mamma the youth campers would be well chaperoned. What Mrs. Snoots neglected to say (and I was glad she didn't) was that boys and girls were going to the same camp simultaneously, sleeping in tents in the same place. Innocent as it was, that would not have boded well with Mamma. She would inevitably have yanked my application from the big stack in the minister's office. And that would have been the end of an adventure I was eager to explore. Sally said she hoped we would sleep in the same tent. I wasn't sure that it was a good idea, but we didn't have any tents, and she did.

My first experience at camp was not what I thought it would be. It was geared for the congregants' different beliefs, and of course, I was not one of them. Unruly young boys scratched on our tent at night, just to hear us scream. I didn't know any of the camp songs, and the ghost stories gave me the jitters. Young girls broke the rules and ran in the open air, wearing only their pajamas. I didn't like burned marshmallows or gas-causing beans. I secretly wished I was home with Mamma and David.

But despite the strangeness of the camping experience, the dirt, sunburn, ants, and mosquitoes, I did my best to be gracious and appreciative of the strangers who kept us safe from wild bears and demons. Mamma definitely would not have liked knowing we were in danger. I was sure she'd never eaten cold pancakes or charcoal-black marshmallows on a stick.

Under the starry sky, I thought of home and my family. I hoped David was taking good care of our toys and Mamma.

Sally said her camping experience was fantastic. She didn't mind burnt eggs, the heat, or the fine, powdery dirt. I was glad she had fun. But I decided to rough it at home. That was a much better summertime activity for me, and thereafter, that's precisely what I did.

I didn't see much of Sally in the following years, and one day, a large moving van parked in front of her house. The workers were too busy to chat. But when the truck was fully loaded, it headed down the hill to another life. The Snoots' car followed closely. It was packed to the roof with chicken crates. From the back seat, Sally's face seemed older, sadder. It was plastered to the window, but she didn't seem to mind. Her head turned slowly as she stared at me—and I at her. I knew far more about moving than she did, and I wondered if we'd ever meet again. I waved at her and hoped she'd find another friend in her new life—someone who'd appreciate her uniqueness with patience.

The corners of her mouth turned slightly upward, and she slowly waved, just as she always had.

CHAPTER 35

Popcorn and Petting

Castro Valley, California, 1952

When shoving off, the chief's dialogue was predictable: "Be good and mind your mother." And when he returned, as though rehearsed, he always said, "My, how you've grown! Why, I hardly recognize you!"

That was an understatement. Indeed, as years passed, we grew taller and less dependent.

It was just as predictable for the chief to come and go—the military's version of family life. Each time the ship moored nearby, we hurried to meet it. And somewhere between the pier and home, Mamma handed over the invisible reins of the head of the family. She knew it was her turn to rest from the duties of being both parents—for a time. Her happy grin said it all: "It's your turn, dear."

It was a few months after my eleventh birthday, over a big kettle of popcorn, when the chief became anxious about living up to his mantle of fatherhood. For some silly reason, he assumed it was time for the proverbial grown-up father-daughter talk that sooner or later comes to every family. The first clue was the constant whispering going on between the two parents. David and I began to whisper too: "There must be about a new stash of candy hidden in some new place!"

We checked all the secret places where they might have hidden a box or two, but none was found. Mamma was never keen on sharing chocolates anyway. And since no one seemed to want to discuss the matter with me, I shrugged and gobbled another handful of popcorn, sharing a few kernels with the dog.

She was my best friend, Jiggers—a little black terrier. It didn't matter that she was just a little black mutt. I discussed everything vital with her. It didn't matter that she was old, itchy, and deaf.

She'd been ours since the last deployment in Seattle. When the assignment was over, Mamma had said Jiggers could go with us to San Francisco if I took responsibility for her. The dog and I were inseparable. Her skin allergies drove her nuts. I knew that she appreciated my gentle touches, and occasionally I gave her a little smooch to let her know she was loved. Poor old Jiggers. She groaned and rubbed her backside on anything that didn't move. Just a few minutes of scratching, gentle conversation, and some petting made her day. Though she belonged to the chief, I was in charge in his absence. I didn't bother to tell anybody but Jiggs, and I knew I was her real owner.

I was the one who fed and bathed her in the backyard. She danced in delight, and we both laughed at her antics. She was a true friend and never grew tired of my stories. As the years passed, Jiggs's girth became as round as she was tall—and she loved popcorn.

One fateful evening, the chief—who wasn't much of a "let me give you hugs and kisses" kind of father—left his comfortable chair and snuggled next to Jiggers, the popcorn bowl, and me. Mamma sat across the room, quietly watching with a different kind of expression on her face. It seemed she was waiting for him to get to the point. I, of course, wanted to get to the bottom of the popcorn bowl before anyone else.

When the chief began talking seriously, using sort of a silly baby tone of voice, I tried not to chew loudly. I didn't want to miss a word he was saying and hoped the terms would finally make sense. The odd subject matter had something to do with kissing and petting, but the conversation was somber and uncomfortable. It was easy to see the poor chief was totally out of his comfort zone.

I wondered if he was feeling well. From the very start, he did not make a darn bit of sense. But as he and Mamma exchanged eye contact,

I had the feeling she was waiting for him to get to the point. Frankly, so was I.

What was this kissing thing all about? He always kissed us when he was going to sea and again when he returned. Was he trying to say I was too big for kisses? Things were even more awkward when he changed the discussion from petting to babies!

What did popcorn or petting have to do with babies? And what did I care about petting? I petted Jiggers every time she looked at me with her blank, needy eyes.

The conversation with the chief was going nowhere, but I listened to his words attentively. They seemed to bespeak of some profound, dark mystery. He asked me the same questions over and over. I kept giving him my most sincere uh-huhs and agreed with him when I thought he wanted me to. I never did understand what he meant to say, and it missed the mark. I had better, more understandable conversations with Jiggers! When the talking concluded, the chief and Mamma were still exchanging strange looks in silence. They didn't say a word until Jiggers and I left the room. Then I could hear them whispering.

Later, I gathered the popcorn bowls and left them in the kitchen sink, thanking the chief for the nice treat. I went to my room to practice the piano, and Jiggers followed. She stood there, staring at me.

"No, Jiggers, I can't pet you. You'll just have to itch by yourself."

I was still reminiscing about the talk and Mamma's strange silence. Was there something she might have wanted to say? As the popcorn disappeared, the chief winced and uttered a lot of useless, enigmatic rhetoric. It was confusing—but Jiggers and I paid close attention anyway.

With popcorn still stuck in my teeth, I dismissed myself from the sofa and wandered into the bedroom to practice lessons on the faithful old piano. Jiggers sniffed at the air, and I told her again, "Somebody else is going to have to pet you now. I'm growing up, and the chief would not like for me to disobey him."

She craned her neck to look at me and then curled her itchy self into a ball at my feet.

Poor, poor Jiggers. I hoped she understood, but I was confident she did not. How could she? I didn't comprehend it either, but I was eager to obey.

To appease him, I didn't pet old Jiggers or the cats for a whole week. Che-Che was not happy when I told her I couldn't pet her anymore. She rubbed her sweet little head against my hand and begged with those big, pleading eyes. I finally gave in—sure the pets would never tell.

I thought about discussing the conversation with my other friends, but it was too confusing and silly to repeat the words. I tried to reason why, all of a sudden, the petting rules changed. I tried to remember his words, but they seemed so senseless. It was something like: "Egos and olio, petting qwerty boys Hoja, ado kissing we le facile!"

"Uh-huh," I uttered under my breath.

And thus, my first diplomatic lecture on the art of growing up took place with a bowl full of popcorn, two confused parents, a patient dog, and two Siamese cats named Su-Ling and Che-Che. Weeks later, the conversation was a thing of the past. The chief returned to the ship, and I resumed all my former habits.

Old Jiggers was delighted, and Su-Ling never told a soul!

CHAPTER 36

Bodacious Nanna

Oakland, California, 1945

The mirror of honesty can be brutal when it whispers friend or foe. For the first time in her life, Ruth saw her reflection in the teary eyes of her grown and wounded sons. Whisperings of the spirit said, "You did that!"

But it was more than bruises, abandonment, thoughtless words, and reckless deeds that brought Ruth to her knees. It was the truth—and an innocent, tiny baby babbling in her crib, helpless and trusting. Ruth was stunned. She felt the overwhelming needs of another person for trust, love, and caring—unfamiliar tuggings of the soul she couldn't ignore and didn't want to see or feel.

How was it possible for her to have brought two precious sons into the world and, staring into their cribs, holding them in her arms, not to have felt a mother's overwhelming love? Life had always been about Ruth—her wants, her needs—never theirs or anyone else's. She pondered, wondered, when was it too late to say, "I'm truly sorry," to change, to stop grieving endlessly for the foolish past? Ruth had extreme difficulty accepting the simple truth: it's never too late—but undoing the brutal consequences of one's thoughts and actions is an entirely different matter.

Ruth stood silently. Looking into the happy face of her first grandchild, gooing in some mystical language, she fell hopelessly, eternally in love with the little one named Nancy Lee.

Had Broadway known Ruth—or Nanna, as we knew her—the question might have been, "Who was Auntie Mame?" Flamboyant, unconcerned with living "properly" or as expected, she did her own thing! Simply put, she was bodacious!

But there was only one star in my world, Nanna. She loved parties, dazzling dresses, large, floppy hats, soft bonnets, high heels, glitzy jewelry, and feathery wraps. She was a free spirit who encouraged others to kick up their heels and live! Like a pied piper, I marched carefully behind, observing and mimicking everything she said and did. It didn't matter that I was only three and she was four-times married and forty-three.

She suggested we sing as we skipped through life, and I did. I sang because she put a song in my heart. She said I did the same for her. I was nearly four when we debuted on her front porch. At the top of our lungs, we belted "Three Blind Mice!" It was our favorite song. Together, we crooned and jitterbugged with total abandonment. The whole world was our stage. After our performances, we bowed modestly to nature's applause. Our appreciative audience included Beebe, the most beautiful and talented collie dog in the world, dozens of chirping birds, and humming bees.

Nanna often played dress-up with me. Her long, flowing gowns, wobbly heels, scarves, gloves, and jewelry were ours to enjoy. Why we even out-Mame-ed the sensational actress and dressed ourselves like two big dolls, lipstick and all. We celebrated in her backyard with tea parties and homemade cookies. Even the sunshine was brighter when we were together.

But occasionally, in the middle of our merriment, tears streamed from Nanna's eyes. They leaked for unexplained reasons. I blotted them with a tissue she kept in her pocket with the candy mints.

"There, there," I said. That's what Nanna told me when I cried.

Ever so tenderly, we kissed, and she said I was precious. Her big, brown, misty eyes looked into my soul. She meant what she said. I hugged her neck and kissed her until she smiled. Begging to know why she cried, she said something about wishing her past had been different, about being a better mother. I didn't understand her words, but I knew she was a dynamic grandmother!

She was medium-old, and it was hard to imagine she'd ever had babies. But the chief assured me she was his mother and Uncle Jon's. Nanna had wished for a little girl. Instead, she had two fine sons, but she was too immature to appreciate them. I asked what they were like at my age. More tears filled her eyes. I guess she didn't remember or want to discuss it.

Occasionally, Nanna smoked long, thin cigarettes from an even longer cigarette holder. Mamma said she wanted attention! The holder didn't bother me, but wide-eyed, I observed her when she waved it in the air. An awful cloud of smoke followed her, burned my eyes, and caused coughing spells and a foul-smelling haze. The smoke was especially nasty in her tightly enclosed sedan. When she learned her habit made me ill, she hastily changed. It was apparent she loved her "favored granddaughter" and "didn't like it one bit when anyone was sick, especially her little Nancy."

With regularity, she visited our home, always with candy tucked deeply in her pockets. Mamma frowned and said sweets spoiled my appetite. The candy was often already on the way through the digestion system long before the bilateral, analytical dissertation between the two ladies was complete.

Among her better traits, Nanna was a serious gardener. She pruned, clipped, snapped, and grafted. As I worked beside her, Nanna described several horticultural projects that piqued her interest. It was as if she and the plants were friends. We walked daintily among them, sniffing and admiring their beauty. She knew the names of every flower. Warmly, she curtsied. "How do you do, Miss Purple Pansy? I'm glad to meet you, Misses Gardenia and Lilly!" Nanna confessed she was working on an extraordinary project; it was a hush-hush thing. She said I had to be patient before she shared it. "The best surprises," she alleged, "take time."

I forgot all about her surprise, but she happily divulged her guarded secret when she was ready for show-and-tell. One beautiful day, she asked Mamma to "dress little Nancy in her prettiest dress—and bring the box camera" to her house that afternoon. There was to be an exciting meeting in her backyard. Mamma grumbled and rearranged her plans. Hurriedly, she pressed a Sunday-best dress and located a pair of small, black patent leather shoes. "Stay clean!" she ordered.

Mamma was seldom late for anything, and when we arrived in Nanna's backyard, dozens of unfamiliar people were admiring her beautiful roses. Beaming, she introduced us to her friends and requested attention as she unveiled her shielded surprise. It was just another rose bush. She snipped a beautiful, long-stemmed flower as the crowd ahhed. She also removed a few thorns and presented the rose to me. She confessed she'd been grafting for quite some time, carefully crossbreeding until she brought forth an original variation. Her wide smile was well earned. The local experts applauded and agreed the rose was unlike any they'd seen. Nanna proudly displayed her creation to other professionals. Unanimously, they concurred her plant was original. Asked what she intended to name it, she replied in her southern drawl, "Nancy Lee," after her only granddaughter. Fellow gardeners applauded loudly and snapped pictures of the three of us, Nanna, the beautiful rose, and a smiling knock-kneed little girl. The club presidency recommended a photo and writeup of the new Nancy Lee. She intended to feature the story in subsequent issues of the *Gardener's Gazette*.

Irritating bees buzzed annoyingly, unaware we were famous! It was a fantastic day.

Nanna was always groomed meticulously. She preened in front of a large mirror on her dressing table. I watched and chattered incessantly as she applied her makeup. Her dresser drawers were bottomless pits of magical mixtures, promises of eternal youth. She said we were beautiful! A girl was never too young to begin beauty routines. Throughout the day, she periodically rechecked the mirror to ensure the magic was still working—and applied fresh lipstick again. She was very concerned about spots and freckles. Her routine promised youthful joie de vivre. Yes, Nanna had face paint down to an artform. My reflection greatly resembled hers. She and the mirror said we were twins, separated by three generations. "Someday, young lady," she predicted, "you'll be glad you took time to care for yourself. You don't want wrinkles, do you?" I checked the mirror. Not a crease in sight.

And Nanna was generous with her trinkets. We stacked pearls, chains, and anything that glittered around our necks. When I thought I could not wear another bauble, she clipped a pair or two of dazzling earrings on my lobes. She said we were stunning! Grinning, I clanked and swooped around the room in her best satin robe.

One evening, Jay, Nanna's fourth husband, came home earlier than expected from a long, tedious business trip. He had no children of his own but sat quietly and watched as Nanna and I discussed the events of the day.

"Oh Lordy, Lordy, Lordy." He yawned. His sleepy, rolling eyes made me laugh.

Nanna liked him. I know because I asked her. I was glad she didn't ask if I did. She looked puzzled when I inquired if she really liked him. She answered with a basketful of complicated phrases. Jay was better than her last husband, she replied. He tried to stab her with a pair of scissors! The thought of anyone chasing my Nanna was unimaginable—but even so, he was a better companion than Jay. Nanna never knew Jay chased me with scissors of another kind, caught and carved his dreaded name on my soul.

I asked Mamma if she liked Jay. She said he provided a good living for Nanna. That was confusing, but it seemed to be relevant to them. Mamma didn't want to elaborate and shooed me away to amuse myself elsewhere. "Run along and play," she said.

Money talk was Jay's favorite topic. Mamma thought he was rude, repetitious, and boring. He didn't have much depth, but chatting about money brightened his face. He had an unusual interest in Mamma and thought his financial babble impressed her.

I began repeating Jay's well-worn phrase, Lordy-Lordy. Mamma didn't appreciate "that kind of language" and wanted to know where I heard the expression. I told her it was Jay talk. She said not to repeat it. "That word does not belong in your vocabulary, and unless you like the taste of soap, you won't repeat it!"

Jay repeated the phrase in Mamma's presence. She frowned. He grinned, looked at her, yawned, and repeated it.

"Listen, Jay," she said sternly, "Lord is a sacred word in our household. We use it in prayer, and I'd appreciate you not using it in vain when Nancy is listening." He never sought the approval of anyone, least of all Mamma. Jay was blasé and muttered something about meaningless words. She said that one meant plenty to her. Of course, he continued to say whatever he pleased. Remembering the nasty taste of soap, I pretended he was praying and uttered a soft "Amen."

Jay's at-home routines were very predictable. At 7:00 a.m., he sat at the breakfast table, poured himself a large bowl of flakey cereal, added cold milk, and crunched noisily. He ate a whole box of cereal every day. Nanna kept cases of it stacked nearby in the pantry. He read the morning newspaper, slowly emptying and refilling the bowl. I wondered about the words running through his eyes.

When Nanna was in the kitchen, I sat at the table with Jay, watching, eating my little bowl of cereal in silence. His mouth opened and closed like a Christmas nutcracker as he crunched the tasteless, cold food. When the box was empty, Jay grinned, insisting I walk to the garage with him to dispose of the cereal box and old newspaper. Though I resisted, Nanna encouraged me to walk hand in hand with her husband while she tidied for the day. She said he (the worst of all students) needed to learn to be a grandfather. He concurred, grabbed my arm with his big, rough hand, and grinned wickedly. Sometimes he picked me up and carried me to an awful fate. Occasionally, Nanna wondered why we were gone so long. Angrily, she pounded on the locked garage door, demanding admittance. I asked why she couldn't or wouldn't see through his transparency. Jay usually sensed when Nanna was suspiciously eyeing him. On those occasions, his behavior was silly and edgy.

In the evenings, Nanna held me in her arms and asked me to kiss Jay good night.

He said, "Oh, Lordy, Lordy," rolled his eyes, and made me giggle. He feigned kindness, but I knew for sure he had a loveless heart. And no amount of coaxing made me call him grandfather! He was never the person anyone thought he was, but he was a fair actor most of the time. However, I always knew God was never fooled, not for a moment!

Few knew Jay retired to his locked garage as often as possible and read dirty magazines hidden among his tools. He was nervous and elusive when Nanna rapped on the locked door. Though she might have been wary, she didn't know the extent of his evil. I wrapped Jay's secrets in privacy. He said if I didn't keep quiet, I would never see Nanna again. And one day, thankfully, the deception ended.

Interested parties sympathized and were assured Jay always kept his affairs in proper order, especially when it came to money. But even on his deathbed, he lied. He'd been dipping into their retirement accounts for years and left his wife penniless.

Nanna was shocked! "Don't you worry, Mom. We'll always take good care of you," said the chief. Jay's death certificate read: Cause of death—prostate cancer. "Fitting," I said aloud, knowing his illness was painful and prolonged.

The chief helped his mother muddle through altered financial records and penniless bank accounts. Not surprisingly, even the vault was empty. The naked truth was there were no assets. Jay secretly liquidated insurance policies, retirement funds, and savings accounts—and spent every cent on his selfish lifestyle and unknown personal interests.

Sudden widowhood without any means of support was frightening. Traumatized, confused, and completely broke, it was dreadful to have been deceived by a man no one really knew. But her faith and ours was comforting. Assurance revealed that Jay's dirty secrets await adjudication in a much higher court where deception is not possible and individual deeds are exposed; a place where no one gets away with anything and the worst of societal miscreants shudder in horror.

Nanna moved into her son's modest home, and he reassured her she was no trouble at all. He never complained or said an unkind word. Neighbors regularly visited, bringing cheerfulness, fresh flowers, plates of cookies, and much-needed lady chatter. It was ironic that the chief taught and cared for his mother far better than she had ever cared for him. But he smiled, kept her tidy, and surprised her with the latest concoctions for her lovely great-grandmotherly face. When she was too infirm to continue her beauty routine, the chief took over.

"There, there," he said. "Smile pretty for me—and no more tears!"

Sadly, Nanna suffered a debilitating cerebral hemorrhage requiring full-time professional care. Her son visited with her in a nursing facility nearly every day, but she was never unable to utter a sound. Her sad eyes followed him as he moved about the room. She waited, and he brought and arranged (and rearranged) bouquets of pretty flowers for her. He spoke as if she were a child, and he her doting father. He held her hand and combed her silvery white hair. Gently, he washed and creamed her aged skin. He promised he would always be there for her.

"Don't worry your pretty little head 'bout nothin', 'specially the past," he softly whispered. "I know you're thinkin' 'bout it, cuz you cry—but it's over. You was just too young to get married and have kids. Bury the memories, and don't think about 'em anymore. Jon and me, well, we forgave you a long, long time ago, Mom. Don't go there …" She couldn't talk, but she could cry—and did.

It was devastating to hear Nanna suffered another massive stroke. "Most likely, she will not recognize you," the nurses warned. They said she couldn't walk or talk and had great difficulty communicating. The prognosis was not good.

Eager to see her after a lengthy absence, I quietly entered her small, sterile room and sank uncomfortably into a chair near the railing of her bed. I thought of the bliss we'd shared. And I wondered if too many years and too much trauma passed for her to recall those extraordinary days. So I simply watched her sleep. She was exceedingly weary. In my mind's eye, I remembered her dancing with the little girl she loved, and I saw her future in death.

Nanna wasn't expecting my visit. Through the years, I made lots of excuses for staying away, but the truth was I never trusted old Jay. Time and too many traumatic memories took their toll. In my absence, Nanna sent letters with pictures of her well-groomed yard, banks of colorful, blooming shrubbery, and swaying palms. I wrapped all of her letters with a pink satin ribbon and treasured them. The dark blue ink has faded, but sweet reminiscences of her are eternal.

When Nanna awakened in her hospital room and found me hovering next to her, I greeted her tenderly and held her soft, limp hand. Her mouth dropped, her eyes widened, and she stared in disbelief.

"Hi, Nanna. It's me, Nancy."

She suddenly jolted out of her dreamlike sleep, sat up, and instantly recognized her now-grown, once-upon-a-time most favored granddaughter.

"Oh, Nancy," she said with love.

Nanna's voice was strained but unmistakable. Her eyes and hands latched onto mine with power and the deepest of emotions. Startled attendants ran for a supervisor.

Her loving thoughts were expressed through worn-out, weeping eyes, tears of regret, and loneliness as her gaze riveted to mine, words she wanted to speak but could not. I smiled, kissed her aged hand, and told her how much I loved her. Knowing she would ask, I said I was fine. I didn't tell her that the only person in the room who was not fine was her.

There were so many things Nanna wanted to say, but the only word she was capable of uttering was my name. It was the last word she ever spoke. Late one evening, she slipped into a peaceful coma and passed away. I like to think, if she could have spoken, she'd have said, "I'm tired now, and I'd like to rest." I deeply regretted anything had come between us, particularly a disgustingly foolish man—and the elusive stranger called time.

"Oh, Nancy …"

And I would have replied again, "Dear, dear Nanna. Thank you for teaching me to sing through life. You were my sunshine and will be forever. I've missed you."

CHAPTER 37

Wooden Marshmallows

Sacramento, California, 1952

Nearly every family has them, the teasers and the teasees. It so happened that the teased in Mamma's family was little Dona, fifteen years Mamma's junior. The child wasn't as precocious as her peers but made up for it in cuteness and tenaciousness.

Who knows how things get started or why? The sisters called it playfulness. Dona called it downright mean. The sisters' whispered rumor said Dona was a hand-me-down, adopted from gypsies who didn't want her ... and poor little Dona was not really one of them!

Of course, they hit a home run every time the wailing child ran to her mother for comfort. It didn't matter that Dona had dark hair and eyes. Tildy said she was beautiful and as much of a part of the large family as everyone else. The heckling would have passed into oblivion if the girls weren't so bemused and pleased with themselves. After all, they were true Swedish blonds, and Dona, well, she just didn't fit the mold. No matter how much comfort and reassurance Tildy gave her youngest daughter, the blonds whispered she really wasn't one of them. The endgame, of course, always sent the child howling for relief. It worked like a charm.

"If you were really part of our family," the girls mumbled, "you'd look like us!"

Tildy was stern and serious about putting an end to the game, but the older girls knew when to giggle and when to hide; when smiling and simply twirling a lock or two of their blond tresses would set off a thunderstorm. Exasperated, the mother had only to raise an eyebrow for the siblings to feign total remorse. They swooned in complete repentance and vowed never to do it again—until the opportunity raised its ugly head. Then, hugging little Dona in contrived assurances of honesty, they whispered, "Go look in the mirror! See for yourself; you don't look like us because ... you really were adopted!"

Unlike them, the child was always cheerful and eager to please. She couldn't help that she resembled her paternal French-Canadian ancestors. As the years passed, Dona matured into a beautiful young woman with dark brown locks and an exceptionally sweet disposition. But even as adults, the girls continued to giggle at their inventiveness and the youngest of the brood's gullibility.

She was only fifteen when Dona's flirtatious nature gave the sisters new fodder for mischievousness. It seemed a certain handsome young man had become the object of her growing fondness. She told her family his name was Bobby and confidently announced she was going to marry him!

Tildy frowned. Yes, she knew who he was, the kid in church with the silly grin and light blue eyes who paid more attention to her daughter than he did to the sermons. Tildy did her best to dismiss the silly adolescent conversations about their commonalities, sharing the same ideals, solid family goals, and being able to care for, support, and love her daughter forever. All reasoning fell upon deaf ears. Dona was seriously talking about marriage—with that boy!

"No means *no, no, no!*" Tildy bawled.

By the time Dona turned sixteen, she and "that boy" were still sticking to their guns. Dona said they'd been patient long enough and were soon going to be wedded—with or without anyone's blessings. Practically before it began, her search for the perfect husband was over. His beautiful name was Robert the Second, and he was twenty years old. Dona proudly told the world he was very mature for his age ... and quite capable of caring for a wife. After all, he was a high school graduate and had a real job reading meters for the local utility company.

Hoping her family would finally be supportive, Dona announced, "We are going to have the ceremony at the church next month. It will be a forever marriage. Bobby and I are inviting our family and his to attend." The mouths of the wide-eyed older sisters dropped in suspended animation.

"Never at sixteen, young lady!" her stern mother declared.

Not since Elaine dropped a bombshell that she was soon to be an unwed mother—since Lavon came home drunk or Madelaine announced she was marrying a sailor she'd just met and moving to China—had the family faced such a crisis. Eddy, their kindly, soft-spoken father, had a habit of gentle reasoning with his family, and they had a history of listening (and following his advice) most of the time. Why, Dona was the epitome of every father's dream child, sweet and submissive, kind and loving. Eddy hugged her closely, smiled, and whispered, "Now, daughter, don't you think you're rushing it a bit?"

Tildy was livid. She was the family disciplinarian, and her word was law. There wasn't time or room for egregious reasoning! Scarcely able to catch her breath, she grabbed her chest, found the nearest chair, and plopped herself into it. Her face was flushed. Had she heard right? Her baby, her sweet sixteen-year-old, wanted to leave home and become someone's wife, and her father wanted to … reason with her?

"He's not welcome, here!"

"Mother! You don't understand—"

She would have continued the conversation, but Tildy closed the subject with a resounding "No! No meant *no*—not maybe or sometime. It means absolutely, unequivocally no!"

Always the peacemaker, Eddie tenderly interrupted, hoping reasoning would win:

"Daughter, you need more time, more experience with life. You stay in school. You'll need more education. If he's the one for you, he'll still be the one in a couple of years. If you wait, we'll give our blessings." Of course, a flood of tears followed the young girl everywhere.

"No!" her mother bawled with resolve. "Two million tears will not change my mind! *You are too young to get married!* He's much older than you are, and if he really loves you, he'll wait for you to grow up!"

Reasoning with a stubborn teenager was never straightforward, and discussing important, life-altering issues with a weeping adolescent in love, impossible.

Passive Dona began behaving totally out of character. Not once in her entire life had she defied her parents. She never gave anyone a moment of grief until he came along. But on this topic, there was very little room for debate, and none whatsoever for a mutually satisfying agreement.

On the other hand, Bobby's sympathetic family completely agreed with his plans for marriage. His sincerity convinced them she was the one and only, a heavenly gift he would not ignore. Age was of very little consequence. At ages thirty and thirty-four or forty and forty-four, the difference would hardly have been as noticeable as a leaf floating in the wind. But the impetuous youths did not want a postponement, not for six months or even sixteen days!

Bobby hopelessly tried to reason with Dona's angry mother, but she would not listen to a word he said. Sixteen was the issue, not the young woman, his family, or his wishes. Tildy glared at the frustrated young man and her brokenhearted daughter. The angry mother did her best to hold her ground and ignore the tears streaming down young faces.

"I think you'd better go," Tildy said to the young suitor.

With her hands on her hips, she added, "Come back in ten years, if you're still single and can remember the address!" It was never more apparent to anyone that proclamations and resolves were chiseled in granite in the Houghton family.

And then one evening, just as they thought things were cooling between the young lovers, Dona calmly requested a family meeting that did not include Bobby or his family.

She began by saying, "Mother and Daddy, I have something to say, and I would appreciate having you hear me out." She was unusually calm and self-assured. The tears were gone, but her dark eyes were swollen and red. Perhaps she'd come to her senses.

Tildy calmly replied, "Of course we'll listen. We love you, and we only want what is best for you, not just now but forever. Your eternal happiness is crucial to us. Someday you'll realize we were always, always only looking out for your welfare. What is it you have to say, dear?"

Dona had the floor. She looked straight into the eyes of her concerned and curious family. Shuffling her saddle shoes nervously, she calmly dropped the bomb and announced their wedding plans were already set. Tildy and Eddie could give their blessings and attend the small soon-to-be nuptials at the local chapel, or the couple would elope. She confidently showed them the ring and the marriage license and said they already had a place to live.

And so, the burden of tears shifted from the teenager to her stunned and mournful parents.

It was with great trepidation and resolve that both families attended the small ceremony, and Dona's family let her go. Little did they realize she'd picked a winner. The day after the ceremony, the blissful newlyweds headed for Salt Lake City on a honeymoon that never ended. As the years passed, children and grandchildren were greeted and loved by both families. Old wounds mended, and worries dissipated. Together, they shared life's joys and sorrows.

Twenty-some years later, Bob calmly announced old friends were organizing his fortieth high school reunion. Donna was lightheaded at the idea of attending. After all, she'd worked hard to acquire her GED and knew there would never be a reunion of her classmates.

On the night of the event, aging friends greeted one another warmly. Some were surprised to find Bob and Dona just as in love as they'd always been. Divorced acquaintances wanted to know their secrets. Others were just pleased to see the couple still joyfully wedded! Many were glad to know Bob had become a celebrated military hero, a pilot who survived the wars. Like most high school reunions, the committee was eager to recognize couples deserving of unusual honors. An outstanding award was offered to the family with the youngest child. On the way to the podium, Bob, Dona, and friends laughed aloud. It was quite evident she was pregnant again ...

Through the years, Mamma and her family maintained even closer ties, though occasionally they still chided Dona the absolute truth, the gypsies didn't want her—and she really was adopted. The terrible teasing became a roll-your-eyes joke in their grown-up years, but a little peroxide made it clear: Dona, even as a blond, was indeed a choice sister with whom to be reckoned.

During the war years, visiting Dona's family was a treasured experience. Her young children made trips for David and me very exciting. As youngsters often do when visiting cousins, we hoped to share sugary treats of any kind. But Dona sent us to the garden for carrots, fresh tomatoes, oranges, and other fruit still growing on the vines. We, of course, were hoping for ice cream, cookies, or chocolate chips. It took a lot of coaxing for our young cousins to plead our cause, and when they did, we were proud of our teaching abilities.

Dona was surprised at the requests. Her kids didn't ask for those sorts of things. It was evident the little ones needed to spend more time with us; they were trainable. Their mother apologized for not having stocked up on sugary treats for us.

"Hum," she said. "Let's check the cupboard."

She rummaged carefully through the sparsely occupied shelves, searching for kid treats and apologizing for not having "anything good." All she could find, she said, was a bag of old marshmallows. Hoping to loosen the contents, she whipped out the bag and banged it against the cupboard. A small cloud of dust filled the air, but the marshmallows remained clumped together like rocks. She said the grocery bag must have been in the pantry for a couple of years or more! We were glad she had forgotten about the old thing.

"Here," she said. "This is all I have—big, colored marshmallows, hard as rocks!" She was apologizing as we drooled in anticipation. "Take them outside and see if they'll do." She had no idea the treat would be such a remembered hit. Smiling, she continued, "Share 'em."

We entertained ourselves all afternoon on the puffy, petrified balls of multicolored treats. Chipping and sucking on the cushions of delight, we managed to divide the treats one corner at a time, laughing aloud as they made squeaking and scraping sounds on our teeth. We slobbered with passion and found great pleasure in the priceless treats too big for little mouths.

"Clean yourselves up in the sprinklers," Dona said, "and dry off in the sunshine!"

In their senior years, Mamma and her little sister laughed and said it was one of life's greatest blessings, knowing their parents were pleased to have been proven wrong ... though they always maintained sixteen was very young to know one's own grown-up heart. And as for Mamma's kids, they never forgot lazy afternoons in the hot California sunshine or washing away the stickiness of the nearly petrified treats and reflecting upon eternal truths. They don't make marshmallows like that anymore ...

CHAPTER 38

Simply Family

Fair Oaks, California, 1952

"Harold! Harold, wake up. It's just another bad dream. It's over now! You're home; you're safe with us."

The aftereffects of countless battles wounded more than the chief's stomach. His psyche took a ferocious beating. Not even the noise of the boiler room could hide the unmistakable sound of incoming torpedoes. He held his breath and sweated; certain death was calling from the other side of the skin. Hal was never sure how or why survivorship was determined, but he felt confident someone mighty important was issuing orders for his survival. Aboard ship, combinations of luck, grit, fate, panic, and prayer were routinely served as was navy bean soup. Each time the vessel avoided an encounter with the enemy's instruments of death, things changed for Harold.

On land or sea, his complaints of stomach pain were never in short supply. Mamma blamed it on the wars, endless doses of worry and fret. Luckily, a careful diet of spiceless foods and bottles of ugly-tasting medicine temporally coated the problem.

"When you come home for good, things will be different," Mamma promised. However, his ulcers continued to boil. When peace seemed remotely possible, the chief finally received orders for shore duty—in Seattle.

In familiar ways, the family packed up and followed the moving van to Washington. For the first time in our lives, the chief was landlocked. I was eleven years old; David was nine. Cooped up in another village of navy housing, the four of us looked at one another, strangers who shared the same surname. The picture we'd kissed good night all those years was an older, unfamiliar man with frustrating, unreasonable expectations of military respect from untrained youths. We called him what everyone else did, "the chief," but standing at attention for long periods of time or remembering to address him as "sir" seldom happened.

Out-of-control fits of temper, agitation, and startled awakenings in the dead of night intensified. He often shrieked in the dark, swinging at unseen enemies, climbing invisible ladders, horrified by incomings and cramped quarters. Mamma knew when to duck and tackle. When the nightmares subsided, she mopped his sweaty brow and rocked him as they cuddled. Sometimes they wept.

"Go back to bed, kids. Daddy just had another bad dream. Everything's OK."

Late in his career, the navy admitted the chief to the hospital for weeks of careful evaluation. After far-reaching and exhaustive tests, the board concluded, "Chief, you've got bleeding ulcers, and we can't cure them. We're recommending an immediate medical discharge."

Not much was said about the battery of psychological tests, but the chief summarized the entire lot as "A bunch of nuts! What did the past have to do with the pain in my guts?"

And so it was, after twenty years at sea, life turned starboard for the chief—and as usual, we followed. The unexpected prognosis swirled headily about him. It facilitated old wounds of insecurity to surface. It seemed two decades and thousands of salty nautical miles defined the elusive middle-aged man we hardly knew. Separation from a lifetime of regimentation was as enigmatic as anything the chief had ever experienced. Whispered private discussions infused new meanings to family cohesiveness. Change, like bells in the distance, tolled softly, ominously.

"What am I going to do to make a livin'?" the chief pleaded. "How am I gonna feed you and the kids? The navy's been my whole life. It's all I've ever known."

Mamma was a great sounding board. As if she had a crystal ball, she predicted a rosy future, opportunities to catch new dreams and make old ones reality. She'd always wanted a house in the country, on a hill overlooking the world. The chief thought he wanted some farm animals, a tractor, and neat little rows of peace and solitude.

I bounced into Mamma's room with a mouthful of freshly baked cookies and found the chief unusually quiet. He was busy, he said. Not even the good smells from the oven interfered with the tasks at hand.

"Whatcha doin' with your uniforms?" I asked.

Broodingly, he mumbled, "I won't need to be wearin' um anymore. I'm a civilian now."

"Well," I replied, dropping crumbs on Mamma's immaculate wooden floor, "I guess we're all civilians. What's a civilian?"

And so it was that time, and changes kissed us softly and pointed toward an unknown future. The chief was honorably discharged in a quiet ceremony. But he always remained a proud veteran and patriot the remainder of his days. What is there about military life that grafts itself onto the soul and makes perpetual brothers and sisters of side-by-side combatants? The chief left the navy, but the navy never left the chief. Throughout his life, conversations were infused with well-worn expressions of "when I was in the navy ..." He was forever salted and peppered with navy blue dreams and phrases. It should have been the end of an era.

Mamma stood her ground each time he started to slide into the valley of depression. She said relocating again and starting over offered second chances for a new life and unanticipated surprises. That was an honest understatement. Because the chief had been gone so much of our growing-up years, he hardly knew us. He called me sis, or sister, and David, squirt! Collectively we were just "the kids."

Nevertheless, we always knew he reached out for love and acceptance needed by all. Of a truth, there was never any rust on the anchor of his devotion to God and country. He truly loved the Mamma we shared. And their lives were as complicated as any mathematical equation— and ofttimes their relationship as turbulent and tempestuous as any battlefield, for better or worse, in sickness and health, on land and at sea, at war or in peace. We stuck it out together. We prided ourselves on being a navy family, though life wasn't easy. It never is. But navy life was ours, the only thing we'd ever known.

In the timelessness of eternity, with grace and softened hearts, it is hoped we may become reacquainted in endless love and peace, known only as the Foltz family.

CHAPTER 39

Open for Business

Placerville, California, 1959

Hal's eyes were pleasantly opened to a second life as he transitioned from sailor to civilian. Gone were the responsibilities of defending the country with one's life and the real possibility of losing it for freedom's cause. He hoped the ghosts of war would finally leave, but they never did. Perhaps part of him expired with the loss of duty and the uniforms he outgrew. Hal traded medals, ribbons, flags, and rank for a simple title of Mr. Harold Foltz, civilian worker, gentleman rancher, husband, and father of two nearly grown teenagers. It's a shame when time, age, and accidents move their unwanted selves into place just when dreams of a new life are on the horizon. So it was for the chief.

Far from the Golden Gate and myriads of memories, Madelaine and Harold followed a Realtor to a generous parcel of land in the countryside.

"Twenty beautiful acres in the foothills of the Sierras," the salesman gloated. "There's plenty of room for a couple of head of cattle and some chickens."

It didn't take much selling talk for the first-time ranchers to skim over the complicated contract and sign it. The property was just what they had in mind. Hal said they would build the home of their dreams, hoping life would unfold its blessings of a secure retirement and, in the future, maybe a few happy grandchildren. Surely, grandkids would be easier to raise and control than past kids—navy kids, to be exact. Moving through the rigors of teenage-hood with the chief was a severe trial, not for the faint of heart—or gruff-talking, ill-tempered chiefs who commanded immediate submission on their terms. But alas, hope and faith shook hands as the long-sought-after dreams of retirement loomed ever closer.

"You're gonna need some water on this land," the contractor said. "That won't be a problem. I'll have someone out here first thing in the morning."

Sure enough, the well diggers pulled into the pasture bright and early the following day. Little did anyone but Hal imagine that the petite woman could be a hell-raiser with concepts of her own. Convinced water was just under their feet, Madelaine told the drillers exactly where to drill.

"Naw," scoffed the grubby workman. "It's most likely on the other side of the property." But after several expensive digs, the news was not good. Madelaine, not used to being ignored, took matters into her own hands, and a caustic conversation was like dung from a flying cow!

"There weren't no water down thar!" yelled the operator. "We might as well be goin'."

Madelaine rarely took no for an answer, but arguing was fruitless. There had to be water, judging from the scrubby oaks in the field. "Wait here," she demanded.

As Hal and the builders, well diggers, and curious onlookers discussed the serious issue of what to do with twenty acres of dry land, Madelaine returned with a branch from a willow tree. She formed a Y of two attached twigs and began slowly pacing through the dry grass. Of course, the grinning audience thought she was crazy. Suddenly, the mysterious branch turned in her hands—pulling itself toward the ground.

"Dig here," she told the scoffing workers. "Dig here!"

Of course, they laughed. With years of experience in the water business, they argued their case like a mob of slick Washington lawyers. Finally, *that look* and several sailor-sized damn-its convinced the ridiculers they had the moral right to waste her money and their time.

"Roar up them engines," said the smirking foreman.

Down went the drill, and up came the water—gallons and gallons of fresh, pure water. It formed pools and finally a steady stream racing down the hill through the dry, golden California grass, to Harold's amazement.

Amazed, the diggers wanted to know how she did it. She grinned and gave them a three-minute lesson on the surefire, old-fashioned art of divining. The foreman uttered a few good damns of his own and offered her a job on the spot. She didn't disclose she'd read about witching in a library book and decided to give it a try—on the spot!

Over the next few days, heavy equipment crawled over the golden weeds, up and down the hill, until a road appeared. There was no use squabbling with the county about it. It was her property, her street, and the leaders refused to pay a cent for it. Scuttlebutt said many other new homes would be constructed on those sites, and they'd need that road. Madelaine stood her ground, as usual, but the county government turned a deaf ear: it was going to be a private road.

She grumbled, of course, and christened it Costa Lotta Drive because it did. She knew it for a fact because she paid the bill! Parting words to the county: "Keep your traffic off my new road!"

Eventually, the county took ownership but not without Mamma first kicking up a lot of dust. Her road was extended for the development of surrounding properties. But sure enough, it was Mamma who permanently put Costa Lotta Drive on the map. Someday it may be a four-lane highway through a densely populated area. And now the family secret is out. Mamma named and paid for it—with the help of an ordinary willow branch, a little faith in herself, and a library book.

With a paved road in place, the Realtor was happy to sell a large plot of land just uphill from the chief's new house. But nobody mentioned the water fiasco encountered in mamma's fields during the buying and building process. However, when the second new home was completed and the well diggers came to fill the new swimming pool with cold, refreshing water at the familiar construction area, they encountered a slight problem. No water! The well diggers were confident that they had to at least tap into Mamma's bounteous underground river if they dug deep enough.

The Realtor's face went from red to white when the consensus of opinions indicated the new home was sitting on a foundation of solid rock. There was not a drop of water on or under the property!

Useless boreholes didn't lie. Regardless of how many expensive tries or which of the various sites they drilled, the results were the same. Drillers were certain one more hole would produce water. But drilling was expensive and proved fruitless. Exasperation humbled the men en masse—including the new owners of the waterless swimming pool. En masse, they trekked down the hill to Mamma's house, envious of her green carpeted lawns. It was apparent; desperation found a foothold. She happily greeted the familiar workers as well as the skeptical new neighbors and pale-colored Realtor.

No one wanted to believe in well witching, of course, but the workers had seen it with their own eyes! They didn't place any faith in old wives' tales or know anything about how to program a divining rod. But the grinning diggers stepped back, folded their arms, and waited as Mamma trotted through the fields looking for a willow tree. Most skeptical of all was the new Realtor. The workers reaffirmed they'd seen it. Mamma smiled and agreed to lead the doubting Thomases through the fields hoping to locate another old willow branch. When a branch was finally found, she placed it in the Realtor's hands with specific instructions. He wasn't sure he even wanted to touch the thing! The new homeowners said they'd give it a try, but it was to no avail. The crowd insisted it belonged to Mamma. She should be the one to walk on the newly acquired property—with "the thing." The mostly skeptical group walked up the road to the neighbor's dusty yard and surveyed the empty pool. Mamma took the branch and began walking across the property. There was dead silence when the divining rod suddenly quivered in her hands and pointed to the watery treasure beneath the rocky ground.

"There! Dig there, right there!" said the new converts. Mamma smiled as fresh, cold water gushed freely down the hill. The group cheered loudly. Mamma grinned as they proclaimed her "the little lady with extraordinary skills."

"Sure you don't want a job?" The foreman grinned. "I've never seen anything like it!"

Like a dog after a pesky flea, the new neighbors gleefully shook Mamma's hand. "From now on, our pool is open for business! You and your family are welcome to swim here anytime." But we never did.

CHAPTER 40

Cricket Was in Love

She couldn't help it. Each time she saw him, she bellowed! He hugged her soft neck, asked if she'd had a good day—and smiled. Perhaps he was expecting a less intelligent response than hers, but looking into her big brown eyes was almost a spiritual experience. He marveled at her amazing lashes. They were more than two inches in length! She had the most prominent, brownest, softest eyes he'd ever seen, and she stared at him with love!

"I'll get to you, Cricket, when I have time," David said.

He was a teenager bouncing into the house with his school books after a long and tedious day. It felt good to sit at Mamma's table, slurping down a big glass of cold milk and a handful of warm, tasty cookies. Deep in thought, ignoring his impending responsibilities, the boy pondered where to place the old soup can Mamma was saving for him. The new BB gun seldom missed its target. With twenty acres in the middle of nowhere, any old log would do after chores.

Cricket waited patiently, but enough was enough. Knowing David delayed his obligations to her, she bellowed again. If his response was not timely, she added more enthusiasm and did it again. David sighed, knowing there wasn't going to be time for a second or third round of cookies. She didn't care that he was a growing boy. He was trying her patience, and she was demanding his attention. Couldn't he tell the utter was getting heavy? Mamma reminded her son Cricket was annoyed.

He had responsibilities for the new family pet. All day, she walked through the golden grass, rounding the fence, looking, longing, waiting, wondering.

Late in the afternoon, when the school bus finally stopped at the bottom of the hill, Cricket stood at attention. She paced, flapped her long, expressive tail, mooed, and bellowed with increasing anxiety. Her impatience and anguished disposition were darn right embarrassing! A beautiful bovine should learn to be discreet. She'd waited, chewed her cud, paced throughout the long, lonely afternoon, and now Cricket was ready for his undivided attention. He alone was the sole object of her anguish.

"Why me?" he asked.

"I don't know," replied Mamma, "but it's you and only you! From the time you leave for school in the morning until the bus returns late in the afternoon, Cricket is one big, lonely Jersey with an aching heart!"

Thinking he could postpone the urgency in her searching eyes, David tossed the last cookie into his mouth and, with the stealth of a grave robber, slid down the hall toward his bedroom. He plastered himself against the wall of the long hallway, slithering to his room, confident she could not follow his movements. But, from the newly planted yard, Cricket's eyes followed him from windowpane to windowpane.

She knew which of them led to his room. She stopped in front of his window and stared in anticipation. The gig was up, of course, when their eyes met. Saturday mornings were incredibly annoying as the teen dreamt of sleeping late. The cow clomped through the yard and slid her head through his open window. Blinking, she spotted the sleeping youth and bellowed. Oh yes, she was training him well and had urgent plans for his morning.

Mamma wanted shelter for Cricket, and the chief said he'd build her a lean-to. After all, it was only a bunch of boards fastened to one another with a few nails, wasn't it? Cricket didn't seem to mind the less than perfect structure. But as David carried a bucket of warm milk to the kitchen, he mentioned the shed seemed to have a rather ominous incline—and it was only a few months old. The chief, bless his rusty soul, wasn't one to hire for carpentry work, but he put on his farmer overalls and gave it his best shot.

The new countryside life was a fulfillment of Mamma's dreams. She painted the house soft pink and white-washed the shutters. It wasn't difficult to find a carpenter to build a fence around their beautiful twenty acres. Only a few scraggly oaks provided enough shade for Cricket. Poor thing, she didn't ask for much, just a little time to graze, a refreshing drink of water, and at milking time, the only man she ever loved—brother David.

Eventually, the barn became a chicken coop, a real farmer carted the beautiful Jersey cow off to a new life, and David's interests shifted to a beautiful young woman titled Miss Placerville—whom he married and with whom he lived happily ever after!

Who knew a simple word like Cricket would forever bring smiles to the faces of a couple of navy kids who almost adjusted to life in the countryside!

CHAPTER 41

Rusty Anchors

The mind has a way of playing tricks, doesn't it? Sometimes it forgets crucial things and, at other times, remembers the mundane. It was so with the sight of the rusting anchors in the bay.

It had been many years since the old green Dodge had lumbered along the seldom-used highway. Winding and twisting, the road hid the notion we were climbing. The day was just another summer afternoon in the California foothills, dry and windy as we headed to the sea.

Young David and I, bored as usual, stared mindlessly through the windows at the endless fields of golden, waving weeds. Mamma, anxious to reach our destination, squirmed in sympathy. The smell of the sea was in the air, and she knew it. But uncharacteristically, the chief refused to exceed the speed limit. Coastal inlets fanned across the ocean like long silver gloves in the sun.

And suddenly there it was, far below, beckoning the curious and melancholy.

As if surprised by the sudden recognition of a nearly forgotten friend or something akin to a long-lost lover, the chief's eyes widened, and his chin dropped. His complete concentration was plainly on the scenery below. For a truth, sailors reminisce about the sea as if she were alive, vibrant, and part of their very souls.

"Good grief!" Harold exclaimed.

"What's that?" I asked.

Madelaine, in command, as she often was, said authoritatively, "Harold, I think we ought to pull to the roadside now …"

All four doors opened onto the deserted road as David and I ran into the wind, appreciating what Mamma called California Gold on the side of the hill. An unexpected breeze smacked her skirt skintight against her thighs. She leaned into the wind, struggling to keep the checkered fabric a decent length. We laughed aloud as the back of her skirt suddenly flipped over her head, revealing a white silk petticoat struggling to hide her modesty. The chief was deep in thought, or perhaps it was the wind in his ears that kept him from noticing her plight. An unusually solemn expression on his face made it clear: he was very deep in thought.

Harold pondered final orders from the not too distant past: "Decommission and secure vessels …" He had to see it for himself. It was a painful reminder of his life, dangers at sea, the horror of wars, and its human toll. It seemed surreal for his family to be together, huddled in the wind, viewing the spectacle below.

Ahead, the Suisun Bay Reserve Fleet was quickly becoming a graveyard for the finest World War II victory ships the world had ever known. Sounds of the gulls echoed across the sky as we stared at the aging hulls. There was a feeling of sadness and wonder; the old ships nested together as helpless slaves in the salty, rusty seawater. Decomposing castoffs were hideously grotesque. The chief stood at attention and stared in silence as a veil of unwanted ghostly feelings nudged him to the core. Uninvited thoughts of the ignominious dead drifted to the forefront of his mind. Harold shifted uncomfortably. He whispered under his breath, "That ain't right. Them ships …" His voice trailed into the distance.

"Nobody'd believe," he muttered, "the things that drifted past those hulls; the pillage, noise, destruction, and anger."

He shuddered again and looked away, knowing eradicating thoughts of hostilities was as impossible as denying the sight of the anchorage below. Uninvited memories continued to dance like actors on the stage of his mind, always fresh, never aging, and refusing to leave, daring old wounds to heal. Seasoned warriors know the atrocities of war leave permanent scars on the soul.

Corroding circles of rust in the silver bay gripped the massive hulls like orange gore. It seemed the fleet awaited commands that would never come. Unkempt battle-gray shells—phantoms of the past—awaited a slow and certain death. Though dignity embraced desertion, neither was capable of consoling the other. The sea was still, a stark contrast to the windy hill on which we freely stood. The wind parted the high grass, and the four of us ambled down the hillside.

Inquisitively, I asked, "Why are those big ships just resting in the water? It's ruining them."

"Where's everybody?" David inquired. "Where are all the sailors, and who's taking care of the ships?"

The chief was silent, but he knew.

Yesterday's warriors traded barbs of swabbing the decks, polishing brass, chipping old paint, and keeping her pridefully shipshape. How dissimilar the old ships below appeared. Once-lofty masters of the sea, these remnants were only shadows of their former selves. In truth, the corroded ladies once served their country as proudly as any navy in the world. Stable, courageous, and unsinkable, they were the best Rosie could rivet.

Why, I wondered, was no one tending to the needs of those noble relics? They seemed so forgotten. Eerily immovable, the once-powerful ships floated alone, unattended—stark reminders of the past. It was as if they were holding hands—ship after ship—alone and forgotten, disintegrating into the base elements from which they came.

The chief sighed pensively.

"Well, sis," he answered at last, "the navy had to put them somewhere, and I reckon this is as good a place as any."

"But," I replied, "the salty water's ruining them. Can't somebody paint and clean 'em up? It looks like nobody cares!"

The truth was nobody did.

Forgotten by time, unnumbered crews lamented the inevitable fate of the aging fleet. No loose lips were sinking these ships; the sea was reclaiming them. Although occasional travelers and casual observers gawked at the pathetic sight, they never saw what the chief did. He identified many, recounting meritorious service, battles at sea, and faithful crews. From scrupulously groomed masts and decks, American flags once whipped proudly in the crisp sea breezes. We stared intently at the graveyard below. It was as if time dismissed thousands of cries, unsung heroes, and marched into the past. Uncaring, she abandoned the fleet to dissolve slowly, alone in the salty bay.

"I think we should go," Mamma said.

The faraway look in the chief's eyes bespoke volumes. He was never far from the ghostly visions and sounds of war. They clung to his soul as tightly as any sailor's tattoo.

The chief's shirt fluttered in the wind as we piled into the old Dodge and rambled off into the future, past glorious reminders of another time. Lest we forget the price of freedom, courage, and bravery of servicemen and women who fought gallantly, the sight of the rusting reminders in the sea below attached themselves indelibly to our minds.

Not unlike the rusting hulls, the chief's military service had come to an end. He'd given Uncle Sam twenty-some years of his life, and ours. He hoped a world at war was a thing of the past, but only the future knows. Harold had seen and lived through unbelievable cruelties. In retirement, forever landlocked, he envisioned himself as a gentleman farmer existing somewhere in the countryside in an environment of perpetual peace.

Long ago, on that quiet hillside, we joined hearts and wished for better tomorrows, remembering the price the chief paid for our right to stand on Freedom's Hill. Oh yes, he paid dearly; and we also, as did countless other families like ours. We never doubted our sailor-father would return home one day, but it never occurred to us how different he would be—how difficult the shift in roles would be for all of us. We couldn't have known how much war changes everything.

The chief's most challenging grappling was his inner struggles with the past, the present, and our future. He'd served bravely and did his military duty admirably, but addressing his responsibilities to the family he loved were yet to be recognized.

Oh yes, war and time changed everything. By the time the chief's beautiful bride reached her middle years, she hoped to work with him in his new role as father and head of the family. She planned to redefine alliances—assemble the near strangers in her household into a cohesive, family circle. Who knew she had only one more decade of life in this world?

Thus, the chief was ultimately alone, trying to make friends with the strangers within his own family. He worked hard to develop an understanding of how destructive impatience and a senseless temper were. Trying to show the tender side of himself did not come easily. As a result, the transition from chief to father was nearly impossible. The reality was his adolescent kids were strangers hoping for a gentle giant in their lives. But fruitless trial and errors were recipes for misunderstandings and, indeed, disaster.

One would have been reading fairy books if one interpreted life with teenagers as easy or predictable. Unreasonable expectations for day in, day out family life were challenging. Though well defined by the chief, they were not at all well interpreted by the home crew.

The most arduous and complicated tasks the chief ever faced were the mastery of himself and learning the tender art of patience with immature adolescents. After a lifetime of struggles, the chief's retirement confirmed what he was reluctant to face: scars of the past and insecurities for the future. Not knowing the art of gentle psychology, Harold might have uttered, "Let's talk about this," but he never did. Perhaps some secret part of him refused to acknowledge the truth, even to himself.

Just perhaps, he couldn't understand the reasons—couldn't exercise patience—because he never learned how. As time passed, his children leapt into their own lives, married, and brought children of their own into a complicated but freer world.

Someday, when reason and experiences unfold and are entirely understood by all, there will be sufficient love, forgiveness, patience, and kindness to heal all wounds—real or imagined. Hopefully, we may announce to the universe, "With all of life's storms pressing against our little family, we did the best we could. And we're grateful and proud to say our daddy was a proud, proud man!"

On behalf of the Shipmates
Of the Fleet Reserve Association,
I present this tribute as
A symbol of love and devotion
To our Shipmate.

We, the Fleet Reserve Association members, wish to pay our tribute to a Shipmate who has received orders to serve on the staff of the Supreme Commander. Chief Harold W. Foltz, USN Ret. Sailed through life's cruise, meeting a share of calms and storms, adverse tides, and favoring winds; the ship of life has come to its final anchorage in a harbor still uncharted by mortal men. We who remain do not know the waters there, but we do know the course to steer, and we believe that our Shipmate, setting that course by those beacons that have been given us, has found that harbor safely. To those loved ones whom our departed Shipmate has left behind, awaiting their own day of departure and voyage to that same harbor of eternal mercy, we can only offer our sympathy in this time of separation and loneliness. Many words could be used at this time to describe the sound and outstanding qualities of the one who has gone before, but we of the Fleet Reserve Association sum it up in one word: SHIPMATE. When spoken by the Naval Marine Corps or Coast Guard personnel, that word embodies all that can be said of any Person. Harold was a shipmate.

—Joseph G. Zuccaro
National Chaplain
Fleet Reserve Association